Everywoman's Guide to Financial Independence

Everywoman's Guide to Financial Independence

Mavis Arthur Groza

LES FEMMES
Millbrae, California

Copyright © 1976 by LES FEMMES
231 Adrian Road
Millbrae, California 94030

No part of this book may be reproduced by any
mechanical, photographic, or electronic process, or
in the form of a phonographic recording, nor may it
be stored in a retrieval system, transmitted, or otherwise
copied for public or private use without the written
permission of the publisher.

First Printing, August 1976
Made in the United States of America

Library of Congress Cataloging in Publication Data

Groza, Mavis Arthur.
    Everywoman's guide to financial independence.

    Bibliography: p.
    1. Finance, Personal.   2. Women—Economic con-
ditions. I. Title.
HG179.G78   332'.024   76-11371
ISBN 0-89087-918-4

    2 3 4 5 6 7 – 81 80 79 78 77 76

For Bob
husband, lover and friend
whose confidence and sacrifice made
it all possible.

For Mavis Pitts Arthur
who taught me how to laugh and
love and feel
but most importantly who taught
me to be myself.

CONTENTS

Foreword

There is a myth prevalent in the modern world—"Women control the majority of the wealth of the country." The reasoning being that women outlive men and eventually inherit all the wealth of the men in their lives.

Women do outlive men, but statistics tell us that of the estates over $60,000 in the U.S., only 1½ million are in the hands of women, compared to 2½ million in the hands of men.

Women might outlive men by ten or twenty years but they definitely do not control the wealth. Most control no more wealth than the money they spend at the grocery store each week. Many women are little more than slaves. They work day and night to clean house, cook, wash clothes, take care of the children and the needs of their men—all for no pay, no vacation, nothing . . . only for room and board and satisfaction.

In addition to that job, some 42.3 percent of women have a second job outside the home where they earn wages. Their earnings are befitting of their station in life, menial to the point of embarrassment, in short, "slave wages."

In 1970, 32.5 percent earned below $5,000 a year; only 1.1 percent earned over $15,000 a year. An average income was considered to be about $10,000 to $15,000 a year but only 7 percent of all women working achieved that; 93 percent of them were below average.

Women do not control the wealth. Most of those who work put all their money into the operation of the home. Few keep a portion of their earnings for themselves. They work their eight hours, deposit the check in the joint checking account and come home to cook, clean and wash.

It seems to me that it is time to stop. It is time to cease once and for all being "kept." It is time for us to learn to keep ourselves—to become financially independent.

You may think you can't handle the responsibility, that you don't know the first thing about saving or investing or even banking money, or how to acquire money that belongs exclusively to you. You can—and now is the time to learn.

You already know more than some men do. Sixty percent of married women balance the family checkbook every month. The same holds true for bill paying and food and clothes purchases. Many men just earn the money; it is the woman who decides what it buys for the family.

You do have the basic knowhow. All you need to do is to commit yourself to pursuing financial independence.

This book is meant to help you achieve that goal. It is not intended to be all-inclusive, not even to be exhaustive on those subjects covered. It is meant rather to spark your interest, to kindle a desire to be financially free, to know the joy of being able to make it on your own.

1

The Law and Your Rights

In 1777 Abigail Adams in a letter to her husband, John, enjoined him to "remember the ladies" in the new code of laws he was helping to draft. He did not. And so began a long struggle by women to free themselves in a country that has based its very foundation on freedom.

Two hundred years later, and countless days and hours of frustration for the women who worked so hard to be recognized, the government has finally heeded the plea of Abigail Adams. It has remembered women with laws designed to make them equal, laws that have yet to be enforced.

Equal Pay for Equal Work

In 1964 the Civil Rights Act guaranteed women the right to equal pay for equal work. This means that an employer by law has to pay a woman and a man the same pay for the same work. In 1971 figures gathered for the publication *Women's Rights Almanac* showed that a law and seven years had done nothing for American women on the employment scene. The figures are proof:

Women professional and technical workers earn 69 percent of men's salary income in the same category.

Women nonfarm managers, officials and proprietors earn 56 percent of men's salary income in the same category.

Women clerical workers earn 62 percent of men's salary income in the same category.

Even where women had the most knowledge, based on what they have been forced to do in the labor force for the longest period of time, the clerical field, even there, men's salaries were higher. The Civil Rights Act did not actually make women equal on the job scene. As a matter of fact, they lost ground. In 1956, a

1

woman working at the same job as a man made 63 percent of what he made. By 1970, she was making only 58 percent.

Discrimination is not obliterated by a law unless that law is enforced. Enforcement takes courage. It takes women willing to lay their jobs on the line by complaining. It may mean dismissal. It may mean difficulty in getting another job, but it is the only way.

A Look at New Credit Laws

A woman in 1974 could not get credit in her own name if she was married. This was true for single women as well, in some cases, even if they had high-paying jobs. The assumption, voiced by some lenders, was that women could not be counted on to continue working. A woman could become pregnant, and abandon her job and her creditors at the same time. In other words, she could not be trusted.

Never mind that the statistics have proven that over 60 percent of the bills in a household are handled by women. Never mind that women manage more money than men. It is assumed that the man is the wage earner and, even if the woman does get her hands on "his" cash, she could never earn money on her own.

Much of this attitude may be justified, but it is not just. Women do not have the earning capacity of men, but not because they can't do the job but rather because the employer chooses to pay the woman less than he does a man for the same work. And women do become pregnant. However, it does not follow that they will become "deadbeats" as well.

In 1975 the Equal Credit Opportunity Act became law. Women were guaranteed by law equal treatment when applying for credit. Creditors are not even allowed to inquire whether the applicant is a woman or a man.

The law has opened doors but like the Civil Rights Act it does not actually guarantee your rights. You still must fight for them.

If, for example, you divorce your husband, you can apply for credit in the same department stores where you now have credit. However, you cannot just take over the account; you must begin again. The credit you have now is probably in "his" name only. Any attempt to change the account from his name to your name will be met with rejection. You must apply, just like someone who has never had an account there before. You are guaranteed equal consideration, based on your ability to pay. That's the catch phrase—"based on your ability to pay." Creditors set requirements that most newly divorced women cannot meet. It is not intentional discrimination but it effectively bars women nonetheless.

What can you do if you're in this situation? The easiest thing to do, at least to get started, is to get a co-signer, someone who will guarantee your debt to the store. This may seem demeaning to women who have always had credit. You may be fifty or twenty years old, but if you have never had credit in your own name you must prove your existence to the credit world, and you must start at the bottom.

However, it is becoming easier for women. At least now we are recognized as being alive, thanks to the hard work of a few of our "sisters." Whether we believe totally in what they have done, we all reap the rewards of their struggle.

Many women do not realize the extent to which they are discriminated against until it hits them in the face. They do not know that as late as 1973, ten states did not allow a woman to enter into a contract (Alabama, Arizona, California, Florida, Georgia, Idaho, Indiana, Kentucky, Nevada and North Carolina). That four states' (California, Florida, Nevada and Pennsylvania) required that a wife get court approval prior to entering a business. New York requires that a woman get a co-signer if she wishes to apply for a license from the Alcohol Beverage Control Board. The same rule does not hold true for men. In Kentucky, a woman cannot co-sign a note unless her husband signs also. In Georgia, a woman's property cannot be used by her as collateral for a loan. In five states (Alabama, Florida Indiana, North Carolina and Texas), she cannot sell her property unless her husband consents.

Community Property and Divorce Laws   In four states that have community property laws (Arizona, Louisiana, Nevada and New Mexico), the husband has total control of the property belonging to both husband and wife. This includes any money the wife may earn working outside the home. Her salary is considered part of the community property. In these states, the husband can dispose of all the community property without the wife's consent or knowledge.

It is generally assumed that an adulterous woman is not a fit mother. Many courts have awarded custody of children to the father because the mother was found to be adulterous. The morals of the man are of no particular importance since the "double standard" says that a man may "play" but a woman cannot. Fortunately, new legislation and fair views of equal rights are eliminating many of these antiquated laws.

The Equal Credit Opportunity Act Married women now have an opportunity never afforded women before. They can, as it were, slip through the side door to establish credit of their own. In November 1976 a section of the Equal Credit Opportunity Act goes into effect that will enable a married woman to establish credit in her own name with relative ease. All it requires is a phone call or a note to all those creditors you have accounts with, whether they are charge accounts or open loans. Simply request that all accounts now listed under Mr. & Mrs. be reported in your name also to credit bureaus. Creditors will be required by law to do this on your request. In this way, you can establish your own credit and be well on your way to being financially independent.

Next, establish your own bank account. It does not have to be a large sum of money. Maybe it is only what you have left over from your lunch money (if you are working) or your weekly trip to the market. Whatever it is, it's a beginning. Sock it away a little at a time and soon you will find yourself with not a great deal of money but at least something that is yours alone. If you need it, you know it is there. At the same time, you are establishing yourself as a person, an individual and not merely the reflection of your husband.

To assume that love will last forever, that your marriage will survive indefinitely is not realistic. Statistics tell us that 50 percent of all marriages end in divorce today and the rate is still climbing. Don't count on being the exception. Prepare yourself. Preparation does not mean that you give in to the inevitable; it only means that you are wise enough to recognize the possibility. This recognition can save you pain and hassle when you least need such problems.

Also don't make the mistake of assuming that your husband will provide for you in the event that you become unable to live together any longer. Although alimony and child support are still awarded, in a staggering 87 percent of cases it is only partially paid or not paid at all. Don't assume that you will automatically get a portion of the estate that you and your husband have worked so hard to build. In forty-one states, the husband is considered the sole owner of all money earned by him during a marriage, which includes any property which the couple purchased. The wife's salary, if she works outside the home, is considered a part of the total, under the husband's management. She can no longer prove that it belongs exclusively to her. Thus, she is at the mercy of her husband. He can leave her with nothing but her personal belongings. Find out just what the law is in your state. The worst thing you can do is to believe in the goodness of *anyone* when it comes to money. The only real way you can prepare yourself is to become independent financially. If you know the road, then you will know where the curves are and can be ready should you ever need to travel it.

The Equal Rights Amendment

When it is passed the ERA will guarantee to all the rights to equal treatment under the law. It is an enormous step toward true freedom for all. The law was drafted in 1923 by the National Women's Party at the direction of Alice Paul. It has taken half a century to get serious consideration by the legislature. It states simply, "Equality of rights under the law shall not be denied or abridged by the United States or by any state on account of sex."

In only twenty-four words it frees women; yet it has met remarkably strong opposition, from some women as well as men. Some of the states that have already ratified it are being urged to withdraw their approval. The Rev. Billy James Hargis of the Christian Crusade said of it, "Twenty-four words that will lead this nation to the brink of Hell." Senator Sam J. Ervin, Jr. (D-N.C.) voiced his opposition in this way, "I am trying to protect women and their fool friends from themselves." Others on the Judiciary Committee have commented that the amendment would never get out of committee. "Over my dead body" were among the words used. Only twenty-four words but so explosive as to bring men to arms.

The Equal Rights Amendment has not passed. If the strong opposition continues, it may never pass unless women unite behind it.

Resources

Know and demand your rights. There are several excellent books that will keep you apprised of those rights.

Women's Rights Almanac, published yearly. Edited by Nancy Gager, Harper & Row: $4.95. This unique book consists of an overview of the status of women's rights during the year. There is a state-by-state directory on such things as women in elected political positions, the state's stand on current issues before Congress, women's organizations, employment, unions, education available, marriage and divorce rates, legal assistance available, rape statistics and assistance, and where you can go for help concerning birth control, pregnancy, adoption, abortion, vasectomy, sterilization, VD, child care, consumer protection, alcoholism, drug addiction and mental illness. Also included are the status of Women's Issues as of the year of publication, and a step-by-step overview of the women's movement. It is highly recommended for the woman who wants to know where the state she lives in and the rest of the country stand in granting her rights she should have had from birth.

Sexist Justice, How Legal Sexism Affects You by Karen DeCrow, Random House, 1973; $2.95. A legal look at women's rights. It is packed with information on court decisions and antiquated discriminatory laws that in some cases are still in effect. An eye opener for any woman who has never been able to really figure out what the feminists have been fighting to gain. Karen DeCrow is a lawyer and president of NOW (National Organization for Women).

Impact ERA: Limitations and Possibilities by the California Commission on the Status of Women, LES FEMMES, 1976; $4.95. The result of painstaking research by leaders in a variety of disciplines, this book attempts to bridge the gap between laws and mores. It analyzes *how* the ERA will affect individual rights, employment, education and domestic relationships.

The Rights of Women: A Basic ACLU Guide to a Woman's Rights by Susan C. Ross, Avon, 1973; $1.25. Covers rights under the Constitution, in each state, and the laws as they operate in various areas of concern—employment, education, criminal justice system, abortion, birth control, divorce. Suffers from no Index and scattered question/answer format but complete in covering the legal systems.

2

How to Get Credit

Nearly every woman in the United States has, at some time or another, experienced the frustration of credit discrimination. Some encounter it upon leaving the security of their parents' home. Most find out about it suddenly following a divorce. They have been accustomed to having department store charge accounts, oil company credit cards, bank credit cards and ease in acquiring a loan at the local bank for a new stereo or a car. The single woman usually finds herself stripped of all credit and not likely to get it back without going through the same rigamarole that she and her husband had to go through twenty years before, but with a lot less to back her up unless she's prepared.

You Need Credit

Credit is the American way of life. If you do not have it, you will probably not be able to buy a car or new furniture or even a stereo. And the number of women who could afford to buy a house without credit is so fractional that it is pointless even to consider.

Whatever your financial situation, you need credit.

Credit is nothing more than borrowing. If you are a good money manager, you use it sparingly. There are different kinds of credit. Not all of them allow you to stretch out your bill; some insist on it, and some leave the decision up to you. You can get credit for almost anything you want to buy, from a box of aspirin to a \$40,000 home to a new dress. You can charge a cruise to Mexico, your yearly donation to the church, the braces for your daughter, or a flight to Rome. With certain credit cards and special bank cards, you can obtain a cash loan.

Credit is easy to come by for those who already have it and have maintained a good paying record. In fact, it is often so easy

7

to come by that you can abuse it, overuse it and ruin your credit rating almost overnight without even realizing you are doing it. You can find yourself in debt for as much as a year's salary if you do not use it with care. "With care" may mean nothing more than not buying a new stereo until you have paid off the color TV, or not buying a new dress until you have paid for the last one. It is all a matter of common sense.

Women have been thought in the past of being incapable of having or even acquiring this good common sense. When a woman asked for credit, things like having babies, quitting jobs and sitting home watching TV while eating candy have flitted through the lender's mind. Thus women have been unable to get credit without a battle. Now it is different—at least, that's what the law now says. In reality it is still not easy for a single or divorced woman to get credit. But you *can* get it if you know and insist on your rights.

What the Law Says

Things are different now, or so the law says. Actually, if you cannot meet the requirements set by the lender, you still cannot get credit and there are few women who can meet these requirements. However, the Federal Equal Credit Opportunity Act which went into effect on October 28, 1975 states: "It is unlawful for any creditor to discriminate against any applicant on the basis of sex or marital status with respect to any aspect of a credit transaction."

In simple language that means that:

1. You may not be refused credit simply because you are a woman or single or divorced or legally separated. As a matter of fact, the law prohibits credit application forms from inquiring into your marital status or sex. If you qualify for credit on your own financial background, you cannot be required to have a male co-signer simply because you are a woman.

2. You have a right to know why you were refused credit. On your request, the lending institution must provide you with a written statement declaring the reason for the refusal. You have the right also to request a summary of the material on which the institution based its decision. The law says that the institution must comply with this request within sixty days of the date you were notified of the rejection.

3. You have the right to examine the files of any credit bureau whose report was a determining factor in rejecting the loan request. You have the right to try to correct these files in your favor. More on this in your rights with the credit union, later in this chapter.

4. Your income and savings must be counted in the same way that a man's would be. Lending institutions must also *count alimony or child support payments made to you*, provided the payer of these has a record of consistent and regular payments.

5. On your request, a lending institution must open *separate* accounts for husband and wife, provided the wife can meet the creditor's normal standards. These accounts must be carried in any legal name the borrower requests; for example, Mary Jane Smith instead of Mrs. John Smith.

As of October 28, 1976, *joint* credit accounts used by both husband and wife must be maintained in both their names if requested. In this way the wife can establish her own credit rating—good or bad it will no longer belong exclusively to the husband.

6. You have the right to sue if you are discriminated against. The suit can include actual damages and punitive damages up to $10,000 for each aggrieved party.

The Federal Equal Credit Opportunity Act does not insure that you will get credit. You must still meet the requirements. It does, however, insure you that you will have equal opportunity to get credit.

Getting a Credit Rating

The very first thing you must do to establish yourself as a good credit risk is to obtain a credit file with the local credit bureau. If you are married and make full use of the Federal Equal Credit Opportunity Act, you can get this by merely requesting it from the credit bureau and notifying your creditors to make their credit reports in both your married name (Mrs. John Smith) and your surname (Mary Jane Smith). If you are not married, it will not be as simple but you can do it. The first thing to do is to contact your local credit bureau and find out if you have a credit file. You may; perhaps somewhere along the line, you received a credit card in your name or you may have established credit when you bought some item like a stereo, on time payments. The credit bureau will provide copies of your file for a nominal fee, usually around $5.

What is a credit rating? It is nothing more than a file that includes information on you that might be of interest to someone interested in your financial reliability or ability to pay. It is consulted not only by lenders but often by potential employers. You can just as easily be refused a job or an advancement in your job because of a poor credit rating as you can be refused a credit card.

A credit rating includes the following information: name, address, occupation, employer, earnings, past earning record, marital history, number of children, moving habits, whether you own your own home, repayment pattern—usually expressed simply as "paid as agreed" or "did not pay as agreed"—any court action instituted against you because of past due bills, stores, lending institutions or anyplace at which you already have credit, the approximate amount of outstanding bills.

A credit report is provided by the bureau on request to stores, lending institutions or other companies who are eligible. The credit bureau compiling the report does not make any judgment on your ability to repay a loan; it doesn't designate you as a good or a bad credit risk. That judgment is left up to the potential lender requesting the file based on the information in the credit report.

Starting a File

If you have a file, ask to be allowed to check through it to see what's included. If all your credit references are not included, request that they be added. You may also check to see who has requested the file in the last six months.

If you do not have a file, start one. Ask the credit bureau to begin one in your name. If you are living alone, you probably have a credit rating with the utility company and the telephone company already. These can be added to the file. At least you will have a beginning.

The next thing to do is to actively seek credit at some retail store. If you have difficulty meeting their criteria you may have to resort to a co-signer, at least initially. This may be humiliating to women who have had access to credit for years, but if it is the only way, it is best to swallow your pride and ask a friend who has credit established to be a co-signer.

If You Are Denied Credit

If credit is denied due to a poor credit file, you have the right to see the file *at no charge*. Simply call and request your file from the credit bureau. The law says that they must let you see it. It also says that if there is an adverse report in the file, you have the right to challenge that report. The credit bureau has the obligation to check out the report to verify that it is correct. If the report proves to be incorrect, then the credit bureau must notify the potential lender of the error. If the credit bureau does not change the report and you feel strongly that the report is unfair (perhaps you had a disagreement with a store on bad merchandise and they refused to give you full refund), then you have the right to write a rebuttal to the bad report and have it incorporated in the file. You always have the right to review your file with the credit bureau, whether it is in conjunction with a recent denial for credit or not. If it is not and you're just curious, the credit bureau will charge you a fee (as indicated previously). This fee cannot be any more than what they charge a lender for the same information.

Things the Credit File Cannot Contain Under the law, the file with the credit bureau cannot contain bankruptcies older than 14 years, and suits and other adverse items of information older than 7 years. This includes suits and judgments, paid tax liens, collection accounts, record of arrest and indictments or convictions of crime. These restrictions do not apply to either good or bad reports on loans of $50,000 or more; loans in that amount can remain on your file forever.

What a Potential Creditor Looks For

Applying for a loan is more than having a good credit report. It can mean much more. In some cases, you do not even need a credit file with the credit bureau in order to get a loan if you meet the other requirements. This is unusual but it does happen. You may find one creditor will grant you credit while another will not . . . with both seeing the same background. Each has its own standards for granting credit but as a general rule, all look for the following:

1. *Stability*. How long have you been at your present job? How long have you lived at your present address? Do you own your own home? If you are a transient in both job and address, you are less likely to get credit. How does the lending institution know you will not pack up and leave before the loan is paid?

2. *Income*. Is your income stable? Do you draw a regular paycheck? If you are in a job (such as writing) with a salary that fluctuates from month to month, this may be seen as adverse. How much do you make? Can you afford the repayment amount each month? Your present bills as well as your salary will determine your repayment ability.

3. *Other Credit*. Do you have other loans, credit cards, etc.? What is your record of repayment? Can you afford to take on another monthly payment?

4. *Checking and Savings Accounts*. Do you have a checking account? How long have you had it? What kind of balance does it usually carry? Do you have a savings account? Savings accounts are usually looked on as a sign of stability.

5. *Age*. Most creditors require that you be at least 18 years old. This is the age at which you become legally responsible for your debts. Many department stores, however, will grant credit prior to that since they have found that teenagers seldom default.

What Kind of Credit?

There are many different kinds of credit but those most likely to interest you are credit cards and installment loans. Credit cards come in different types—from those that allow you to charge up to a certain limit, paying only a minimum amount each month, to those that require that you pay the balance on receipt of the bill. Installment loans also come in different types, depending on what you are borrowing for and from whom you are borrowing. Generally, if you are making a large purchase, say a boat or a houseful of furniture, you will want an installment loan. If it is a smaller item, a new dress or rental on a car for a day, then you need a credit card.

Credit Cards   There are essentially three types of credit cards, each with its own features. These are:

The One-Purpose Card   These include department store and oil company cards as well as car rental cards and telephone credit cards. They are any card that can be used with only *one* company. Interest rates are usually 1½ percent a month (that's a yearly rate of *18 percent*). You do not need to pay off the balance each month. As a matter of fact, they may prefer that you keep a running balance; it enables them to collect those high interest rates. With all its disadvantages, this is the most widely used card in America. It's the card you use to buy a new dress or a toy or a new pair of shoes, those little purchases that don't seem like much until you get the bill at the end of the month. With large department stores like Macy's etc. it may even be used for major purchases.

If you let yourself go "wild," you could conceivably end up with a dozen or two of these cards in your purse. Once you have established your good credit, you will find them extremely easy to get.

The Bank Card   The most popular of these are *BankAmericard* and *Master Charge*. Many banks across the country are issuing them today. In some ways they are even more dangerous for your spending habits than the one-purpose card. A bank card costs nothing to acquire, initially, and you can buy almost anything, anywhere. If it's one of these recognized cards, most businesses will accept it. Its use is not limited to any particular kind of store. They are accepted in restaurants, florists, hotels, airlines, dress shops, specialty stores and almost any other place you can name; they can even be used in large cities overseas. Think of what you could do with this card—think also of the bill you could end up with at the end of the month.

A bank card allows you to pay a minimum amount monthly, usually about 10 percent. The size of your account usually is limited to a certain amount. Depending on your income your limit could be $200 or as high as $1000. Interest varies from 1 percent to 1½ percent a month, and you can get cash advances with this card. All you need do is apply at any bank that honors the card. It is only a matter of signing a form and you walk out with the cash.

There is some talk now of banks charging a fee for those who choose to pay their bills in full before the bank has had an opportunity to levy interest charges. You usually have thirty to sixty days to pay before this happens. The banks' logic is debatable. They subsist on the interest rates and if too many people do not give them the opportunity to collect that interest, they must make the money somewhere else, thus the charge for paying on

time. This will, no doubt, be challenged and end up in the courts.
Travel, Food, Entertainment Cards These are specialty cards
designed for the traveler or the businessman who entertains fre-
quently. The "biggies" are *American Express, Diners Club,* and
Carte Blanche. These cards are not free. You pay a yearly fee,
usually $10 to $15. These cards also expect you to pay in full on
receipt of the bill. Some allow for extended payments but you
must arrange for this prior to making the purchase, otherwise it
is assumed that whether the charge is $10 or $1000, you will pay
when you get the bill. Your card will not be renewed if you
disregard this rule.

Use of these cards has broadened somewhat in the last few
years. Where they were once used almost exclusively for restaurants, hotels, airlines, car rentals or florists, you can now use
them in many of the same places that you can use the bank card.

Installment Loans You can borrow money for a trip to Ber-
muda, a thirty-foot sailboat, a sixty-foot mobile home, an additional bedroom for your home, your own jet, a color TV, or a
facelift. Whatever it is you want, if you have a good credit stand-
ing and you can prove your ability to repay, you can borrow the
money to make it yours.

It is not quite that easy to actually get the money, but the
variety of choice is certainly there. The way you borrow can
make the difference between paying for it once, twice or more
times. The less you have to offer to back up the loan in the form
of cash, stocks, property (called collateral), the higher the interest
rates. The higher the interest rates, the more it will cost you in
the long run.

Basically, an installment loan is either *secured* or *unsecured.*
A secured loan is one that has something to back it up. It has
collateral. You borrow money to buy a new car. The car is your
collateral. If you do not pay, the lending institution repossesses
the car. In essence, the car belongs to the lender until you have
paid for it in full. You are only paying for the right to use it. A
home falls into this same category, as do most large purchases
you will make. Whatever you are buying, whether it be a boat, a
mobile home or a stereo, you are using the purchase itself as
your collateral.

The unsecured loan is just the opposite and more difficult to
obtain. The lending institution loans you the money without

"security," on your good credit only. You promise to repay the loan and they accept your promise as collateral. These types of loans generally have much higher interest rates, 17 percent or more, and they usually have very strict rules for repayment. In addition your credit record must be well established and above average in dependability.

Special Types of Secured Loans

Loan Against a Savings Account These can be obtained from whatever institution carries your savings account, whether it be a bank, savings and loan association or credit union. When you take out this type of loan, your savings must be large enough to cover the loan. Say you want to borrow $1000. You must have at least $1000 in your savings. The lending institution agrees to lend you the money with your savings as collateral. They place a freeze (meaning you cannot withdraw the money) on your savings account for that amount. It remains there, decreasing as your loan balance does, until the loan is paid off. This type of loan carries a very low interest rate. Some may be as low as only 1 percent since you recoup a portion of the loan interest on the interest you are earning on the savings account. The advantage to borrowing instead of using your savings is, of course, to retain the savings.

Mortgage Loans Basically these are FHA, VA or conventional loans. They may also be open-end mortgages. Open-end mortgages mean you can borrow money against your investment at some later time without refinancing—say, in five years you have put $8000 in the house, and you want to remodel; with an open-end mortgage, you can borrow that $8000 or any portion of it. If the loan is not open-end, then you must refinance the entire house in order to borrow from what you have invested in it. This can be costly as you must now refinance under the new interest rates in effect, which are likely to be much higher than the rates you financed at in the beginning. There are also fees involved in refinancing which can make this type of loan prohibitive.

FHA loans are insured by the Federal Housing Administration. The insurance is not for you but rather for the lender should you default on payment. Down payments usually range from 5 to 10 percent with payment terms as long as thirty to thirty-five years. There is a limit on the price of a home that can be mortgaged under FHA. In 1973, it was $37,000. The price, of course, changes as property values change.

There can be a lot of red tape to getting an FHA loan, so much that you could lose the house while you are waiting. If you consider this type of mortgage, then send for the following booklet so you will know all the rules before you plunge in: "FHA Morgages," Federal Housing Administration, Department of Housing and Urban Development, 451 7th Street, S.W., Washington DC 20410.

VA loans are available to veterans only. The local Veterans Administration can give you the latest qualifications and terms for this type of loan. It requires no down payment and you can finance the entire amount for as long as thirty years. Closing costs still must be paid by the buyer. As with the FHA, you will run into a lot of red tape, but if you are a veteran and have no money available for a down payment, then a VA loan may be the answer. Remember, however, that with no down payment your monthly payments will be higher. This loan has a limit as to the purchase price of the house as does the FHA loan. The limit is usually the same as the FHA.

A conventional loan is the one most people end up obtaining when buying a home. The loan usually goes through a local savings and loan association or bank and the terms are 20 percent down and payment terms up to thirty to thirty-five years. Interest rates fluctuate according to the country's economy and they are not always the same at all institutions at the same time. You may find an 8½ percent at one place and an 8 percent at another. Shop around.

Where to Get Loans

The decision of where to get a loan is not always necessarily left up to you. If you buy a stereo or a car, for example, you may find that the dealer carries his own financing and that it is much simpler to let him handle it for you. What they do is sell it to a lending institution, usually a bank. Before you allow them this latitude, however, find out where they are going to finance the merchandise and what interest rate you'll be paying. It may be to your advantage to finance it yourself with a bank or elsewhere (as a secured loan) and present the dealer with a check for the full amount.

Places you can get a loan on your own include:

A Life Insurance Policy   If you have a life insurance policy, it may be convertible to cash (see chapter on Insurance). If it is, you can borrow against the amount you have already paid into the policy. For example, if it is a $5000 life insurance policy and you have accumulated $1000, then you can borrow $1000 against the policy. Interest rates tend to be low, running to 6 percent, and in some cases, you do not have to repay the loan. If you do not, however, the face value of the policy decreases in proportion. Therefore, if you elected not to repay the $1000, your policy would be worth only $4000. Also many of these policies pay dividends and these can be withdrawn totally with no repayment.

Bank   The bank where you carry your checking and/or savings account will most likely grant you a loan if you have a good credit rating. Bank loans, if backed by collateral, may bear a low interest rate, below 10 percent. However, if they are not backed by collateral, the interest rate may be as high as 17 percent. Your relationship with the bank will determine how much they will loan you and at what interest rate.

Savings and Loan Association   Generally, what is true for the bank is true for the savings and loan association. Although the savings and loan operates mainly to grant loans and hold savings for customers, it operates in much the same way as the bank in granting loans.

Credit Union   If you belong to a credit union, you will most likely find the lowest interest rate possible there, particularly on a loan not secured by collateral. Women today have an opportunity to join the newly formed Feminist Credit Unions specifically designed to help the woman who is having difficulty obtaining a loan. (See the chapter on Savings for locations in the United States.) Credit Unions operate much the same way as a savings and loan with the exception that loan interest rates tend to be lower and savings interest rates tend to be just a bit higher.

Finance company   If you have tapped all the other sources and cannot get a loan, you will probably be able to get one at a finance company. They are accustomed to the person who cannot obtain money and they react accordingly. You will find yourself faced with exorbitant interest rates and a very strict repayment policy. Be wary of going to this extreme.

Resources

For More Information Write:

1. Your local Feminist Credit Union—addresses in the chapter on Savings.
2. "How to Establish Credit," Bank of America, Box 37128, San Francisco, CA 94137.
3. "Women and Credit," National Organization for Women, San Francisco Chapter, P. O. Box 1267, San Francisco, CA 94101.
4. "Credit for Women," Consumer Credit Association, P. O. Box 2049, Dallas, TX 75221, $.25.
5. "Women and Credit," National Organization for Women, National Office, 425 13th Street, NW, Washington, DC 20004; $3 members; $5 nonmembers.
6. State Commission on the Status of Women. Write to your state capitol.
7. National Organization for Women (NOW). Check your telephone book for the local chapter or write the National Office (see above).

If You Need Help If you feel you have been discriminated against, contact the following special agencies.

Banks:
   Federal Deposit Insurance Corp.
   550 Seventeenth Street, N.W.
   Washington, DC 20429
Department Stores—Credit Cards:
   Federal Trade Commission
   Washington, DC 20580
Federal Credit Union:
   National Credit Union Administration
   Office of Examination and Insurance
   2025 M Street, N.W.
   Washington, DC 20456
Credit Rating:
   Associated Credit Bureaus, Inc.
   6767 Southwest Freeway
   Houston, TX 77036
Federally Insured Savings and Loan Associations:
   Office of the General Counsel
   Federal Home Loan Bank Board
   101 Indiana Avenue, N.W.
   Washington, DC 20552.

Credit is your right In today's economy it's almost impossible to live without it. Without it, you can have difficulty getting something as simple as a telephone or electricity in your apartment. Whether you plan to use it extensively or not, you need it.

3

Budgeting

Living by a budget is not going to be easy, and yet it is the single most important part of becoming financially independent. If you do not know where you are spending your money, then you can't control it. You also can't change any negative spending patterns you are now involved in day after day unless you find out what they are. Only by going through the process of budgeting can you really discover what your spending patterns are.

Remember the allowance you used to get when you were a kid. You never really planned the spending of the money. It just seemed to happen. If you went to the store, you bought a candy bar or maybe you went to a movie. By the same token, your paycheck today is probably going the same way. You pay rent, electricity, buy a new dress, food, a bottle of scotch, whatever else happens to occur when you have money left. Then a bill comes a day too late and it has to wait until the next month.

It is a cycle, a destructive cycle that will eventually fail when you need money most—when you are faced with no money for an unplanned trip to see a sick relative, for a vacation you have always wanted to take, a new outfit for a special occasion, a gift for a friend getting married, a new car when yours dies, or something as simple as buying a steak dinner for a special friend. If you live from month to month, depending on the kindness of the fates to make the money meet the expenses, you are going to fail. It is only a matter of time.

A Checking Account as a Solution

Some look on a checking account as the solution to their money problems. The logic being that you will not spend as much if you do not have the cash. Bad assumption. Checks are very much like cash, and in some ways even more dangerous to your finances.

19

Say you buy a new dress. What would make you feel the loss of the money more, writing a check for $50 for the dress or pulling two twenties and a ten out of your wallet? Writing a check is simple. You don't really feel it is cash, and there is the feeling that your resources are unlimited, that there will always be enough money to cover the check. Then it is possible to start writing checks even when you do not have any money . . . borrowing on your checking account, *if* the bank pays the overdraft, which they probably won't unless you have a substantial savings account with them. Whether they do or not, you end up with a charge against your account for the overdraft, an amount that can be staggering in relation to the amount of the check you wrote. Whether you write a $10 check or a $100 check, the bank charges the same, usually $3 or $4. In addition to the bank charge you will have to pay a charge to the store where you wrote the bad check. This can run as high as $10 for each check, not to mention the ill feelings that the store will harbor against you.

A checking account will not budget your money for you. Its value is in helping you keep track of your spending habits and as a form of receipt. You have to assess and organize your spending, find out where it is going and reroute it if it's going in the wrong direction.

Define Your Problem

What is your major failing when it comes to money? Does it dribble away on frivolous things? If you are like the majority of those with money problems, you have four areas which you must watch:

CREDIT CARDS—The ease of spending with credit cards will get you in trouble eventually unless you are careful. Department stores, notably, will let you charge and charge, letting your balance go as high as $500 or $1000 before they call a halt. And even then, if you are making the minimum monthly payments (usually $10 to $20), they may let your spending splurge continue. Some of the bank cards are even now instituting a penalty charge for those who choose to pay off their account in full with the first bill. They want you to charge and pay only the minimum amount. That way they can sock you with 1½ percent service charge on the balance of each bill. In case you have not added it up, that is, as mentioned before, 18 percent a year. Who wouldn't like that kind of return on an investment. And that, after all, is what the banks and department stores are doing. By, in essence, lending you $500, they are investing it and the returns to them are enormous.

INSTALLMENT PAYMENTS—You want a new car. You can't afford it but you want it. So a car dealer kindly sets you up with a loan to cover the cost. For only $100 a month, it's yours. You don't know where you will get the money but you do it anyway. Or maybe it's a new color TV set or a bedroom set or a dining room table or vacation to Hawaii. You name it, they have a loan for it. For only so much a month for the next five years, you can have what you cannot live without. It never occurs to most people to stop and ask themselves if they want it badly enough to spend month after month for three or four or five years paying for it. How important is it to you? And what about next year— will you add another payment on then? It's hard to say no; the seller knows that—that's what keeps him in business.

FOOD—Everybody has to eat. It is one activity you can't get away from. Some have such a fatalistic attitude about food bills that they do not even flinch when the bill soars. After all, they do have to eat. But do you have to eat the most expensive way? Figure out how you spend your food dollar. Do you live on steaks, expensive prepared frozen food, imported cheese and high priced liquor? Do you shop when you are hungry? Shopping when you are hungry is absolutely the worst thing you can do. You will end up with a basket full of food that you cannot possibly eat within a week, which is the best time period to buy for.

Your food bill basically depends on two things—when you buy and what you buy. You can change the price you pay for food by buying fresh foods in season, planning your meals to avoid the high-priced items—and staying away from the store when you are hungry.

Housing—Where you live determines where the biggest chunk of your money goes. Estimates for housing run from 15 to 30 percent of your income. If you are spending more than that, then you probably can't afford your home or apartment. That does not mean that you must or should move. It only means that you are spending more than you should in relation to your income and you must cut down somewhere else. If the location means a great deal to you, you probably prefer to spend the extra money on housing rather than on clothing or food. It's all a matter of where you place your priorities.

Once you have defined your basic problem, which undoubtedly lies somewhere in the above areas, then you can find a solution. It is very likely, however, that defining it will not be all that easy. If you are like most people, you are not aware of what your problems are because you really do not know where your money is going.

Where Does It All Go?

Statistics tell us that you will earn between $250,000 and $500,000 in your lifetime. They also tell us that the odds are that you will have little or none of that left when you retire. Where does it all go? Like the allowance you got as a kid, it just disappears, little by little, month by month. You can stop—and learn how to keep some of it—but not until you know where it is going. Thus, the need for a budget.

What Does Everyone Else Spend?

In the 1970s Americans were spending the following percentage of their paychecks on the named items:

22% Food, alcohol, tobacco
15% Housing
15% Housing upkeep such as electricity, gas, garbage and telephone
14% Car including gas and upkeep
10% Clothing including new purchases and upkeep of the old
8% Doctor, dental and drug
7% Recreation including vacations
9% Personal expenses

This is an average and not necessarily what you should be spending. On the contrary, no two people are alike in what they need "to make it." You should use these figures only as a base to determine how you want to spend your money.

How to Plan Your Budget

The very first thing you must do is find out how much you have each month to spend. Then and only then can you determine how to spend it. Add up your paycheck plus any other income you might have such as child support, alimony, interest, trusts, second job, etc. It is, of course, pointless to use the figure you actually *make*. Uncle Sam gets a large chunk of that before you even see it. So base your figures on what you actually get in your check. Say you make $800 a month; the amount may be only $600 when you receive it. That $600 is what we are concerned about here.

You know what you have to spend, now for the budget. Start with your monthly expenses *now*. Make some broad estimates using the record sheet at the end of this chapter to assist you. Add additional columns for other expenses you have monthly which do not already appear. If you have made an installment purchase of say a total of $100, enter *only* the amount you have paid on the account for the month, for example, $10. (Once you get an established budget, you can take note of all of your installment purchases and see how much your total debt is.) Use the explanation column to note specifically to whom the money went.

Once you have added up all the monthly expenses, compare this against your monthly income. If the expenses are more than the income, then you need to make an adjustment in the expenses. Something has to go. Make a decision and cut back—*now*.

You have made a beginning when you complete this estimated budget, but it is only a beginning as it is based on inaccuracies unless you have kept an accurate check book. You will not be really certain that your figures are correct until you keep a detailed record. Do that next.

Start a new record sheet. At the top of each column, put the amount of money you have decided you should spend on each item; that's your *budgeted* amount. Each day deduct the amount you have spent in that category from the budgeted amount. It helps to buy a small notebook to keep in your purse and record amounts as you spend. Continue to do this for a month. When your balance runs out in a column, you have run out of money for that item. Ideally, you should not spend any more money there. You may find this difficult, however, if the column happens to be food or housing expenses. There are bound to be some loopholes at first in the amounts you budgeted based on estimated expenses. Continue through the month, and at the end, add all the columns and adjust the budgeted amounts accordingly. Then begin another month.

A column you should not leave blank is the one titled savings. The purpose of the budget, after all, is not only to make the money fit the needs but to save a little, too. Try to put something aside every few days. If you have not ever before saved regularly you will most likely find saving money difficult. Do it anyway. Otherwise, it's all for nothing—financial independence *depends* on saving.

Items You Will Not Find on Your Monthly Budget

Some things not included on your monthly budget sheet that you will have to pay are probably the biggest expenses you have all year. For these you must set aside money every month (use the *savings* column for this) or you will end up having to borrow money when payment time comes. These expenses include such things as income taxes, property taxes, insurance payments, license for your car, a medical bill, dental work. Call this your "money in waiting," *waiting* for the bill. Try to save a little in addition to this amount.

In order to spread these expenses over a year, sit down and figure out how much they add up to, in total. If you do not know exact amounts, check last year's bills and add a bit for inflation. In the case of your income taxes, take into account any money that is already coming out of your paycheck. You can ask for help from the IRS or your company bookkeeper. Maybe you will not need to save any additional for the federal government, but state taxes may be a different story. If you own a home, your property taxes may be already included in your monthly payment. But there are some that you know you will have to pay, like the license on your car or some personal insurance policy.

Add them all up and divide by twelve. This will give you the amount of money you will need to save each month in order to meet the bills without borrowing. You may find you cannot save that much. If this is the case, save as much as you can. Set a goal so that you know when it comes time to pay you will have a certain amount of money on hand. You may have to plan to borrow the remainder, at least until you get your budget working efficiently. Whatever you do, do not omit putting money in a savings account for any reason. You will need it.

What to Do with Unexpected Money

Perhaps you might receive a gift of money, sell a personal belonging, sell some goods at a garage sale, or you write an article; you will find yourself with money not a part of your budget. If your budget is working well, you will not need the extra money to live on, so what do you do with it? The sky is the limit; it's yours. You can add it to your vacation money, buy a new wardrobe, add to your savings or buy a new appliance. It is extra money and it is a bonus to you if you have planned well for your daily expenses through a budget. It is your reward for budgeting. If you really want to become financially independent you'll put it in a high interest savings and loan institution and plan on adding to it—to enjoy spending the *interest* later.

If You Are Living With Someone

If you are working and living with someone in a close relationship, whether it be a friend, lover, or your husband, you will have special budget problems. Who will pay for what? You should maintain your own budget and your own money but you will have to contribute to the daily living expenses as well.

Try this system . . . *Ours, Mine* and *Yours*. First do a joint record sheet as described before. Each month, contribute a certain percentage of your salary to a fund for joint living expenses. From this comes all the expenses that you would normally incur in daily living, *including* clothing and personal toilet items. Include everything but a personal weekly allowance (for lunches, treats etc.) which you keep separately. The percentage contribution is decided by how much the joint budget determines you need for these expenses. Say, you need $2000 a month for living expenses. If one makes $1500 a month and the other makes $1000, each would contribute 80 percent of her/his salary to meet the living expenses. For extra expenses, such as a color TV or a new dining table, each contributes an equal amount. This system allows both parties to establish some amount of money of their own. Even married women can develop savings and establish credit, eliminating their status as "non-people."

Conclusion

There is no set answer to budgeting. Everyone has to work out her own best system. Your circumstances as well as your personality dictate where you spend your money. A fancy apartment may be important to you while I am happy in a tiny studio. A steak dinner once a week may be my big expense while you may relish a visit to the race track every month. A budget is not meant to bind you into giving up those things that mean the most to you. On the contrary, it is meant to help you control your spending on those things you do not particularly care about so you can have money left for those that do mean something to you.

The idea behind budgeting is to know where the money is going and to cut down spending on those areas where it is excessive and unessential. Try it. You may find yourself spending your money where you really want to spend it for a change.

Monthly Budget Record

Date	Rent/ Mortgage Payment	Housing Expenses	Car Expenses	Medical Bills	Installment Payments	Charge Card Payments	Clothing	Recreation Expenses	Personal Allowance	Food	Savings	Explanation

4

Security–Saving

Saving money can be the hardest or the easiest thing you do. It all depends on how you approach it. If your attitude is positive, if you make a firm commitment to save "no matter what," then the chances are that you will be able to do it. If you see saving as a waste of money that you could be spending on fancy clothes or flashy cars, then you will probably get little more than several hundred in the bank before you withdraw it all on a whim and demolish your savings.

Saving money is a serious business, a necessity to combat problems with the "unexpected." Think of it as an investment in the future. What would you do if you needed medical attention and your insurance did not cover all the costs? What if you lose your job?

Financial experts tell us that we should save an amount equal to from two months' to six months' take-home pay before we feel really secure. For some that may seem like an astronomical sum. But it actually can take that much to tide you over an emergency.

And then look at the other side of it. Saving does not have to mean putting money away only for unpleasant happenings. It can just as easily pay for that long-deserved and wished-for cruise, for starting or returning to college; it can be money for a special vacation or even the down payment on that flashy car. The important thing is that you should have a goal, a good reason to save; otherwise you may not succeed.

Using your savings for such special things does not have to mean that you use up everything in the account. You may not even have to touch the savings; you could borrow the money, using your savings account as collateral. This way, you do not have to start over again. That in itself is worth the interest you pay on the loan (which is partially offset by the interest accruing on your savings account). You retain your savings with only the stipulation that you cannot touch an amount equal to the balance on your loan until the loan is repaid. But at least your savings are still there. That knowledge can help you retain that feeling of security.

How to Save

Let's say you have decided to save your money for a pleasant occurrence, say a cruise around the world. First check out the departure dates and make a firm commitment in your mind for a particular date in the future. This will help you stick to your program of savings by giving you a goal.

Determine how much you will need for the fare and expenses, and how much time you have to save that amount. In this way, you can determine how much you will need to save each month to reach your goal. Then, checking your budget, decide whether you can afford to save that much. If not, recheck your schedule. Perhaps you can count on some extra money from gifts or bonuses or a part time job. If not, then you may have to delay your departure time for several months. The main point to re-member is that you should not plan on somehow saving more than you can actually spare from your budget. You do not want to ruin your credit rating by leaving bills unpaid while you stash money away for that cruise.

The best of all possible ways to save is to do it on a regular basis—once a month, once a week, every day, whatever—but regularly. Plan to increase it a certain amount on some pre-determined time schedule. That sum can be as modest as $1 or as large as $100. Being a successful saver means setting aside money for that purpose and using it for nothing else. If, for example, you have $5 in your purse that you plan to put into savings and you do not make it to the bank on the day you usually deposit, chances are you will spend it before you ever get there. If you plan to deposit on the 15th, save on the *15th*. Not being able to make it to the bank is no excuse. You can just as easily deposit by mail or at the bank night-drop after hours.

Other methods you may want to use to save include:
Automatic Deposit from Your Checking Account All banks will transfer funds from your checking account to your savings at a

predetermined date each month. You must remember only to deduct the amount from your checking account on that date. This method is easiest for some people because it is money they never actually see.

Percentage Saving This involves embarking on a plan to save a certain percentage of your money, say 5 percent of every check you receive, whether it be paycheck, a gift or a dividend check. That 5 percent belongs to your saving account. Deduct it from the check before you have a chance to spend it. Chances are you will not even miss it.

Extra Money Saving Any and all money you might receive that is not a part of your regular paycheck, gifts, dividends, tax refund check, any money no matter how small, is put in a savings account. This method will not increase your savings predictably but it will increase your savings, and perhaps in a dramatic fashion. Few people realize how much extra money passes through their hands in a year. That alone may pay for your cruise.

Where to Save

Where you decide to save your money makes a great deal of difference. There are a variety of saving plans open to you, depending on how much money you have to open the account, on whether you will be withdrawing money, and on how long you can afford to leave the money untouched. There are basically three different places you can put your money—the commercial bank, the savings and loan association or the credit union. Each has something to recommend it.

Banks Saving at your bank is convenient. You can take care of your savings at the same time you deposit money in your checking account. Banks also offer the added service of bank by mail and the transfer of money from your checking to your savings automatically. Savings in banks are insured by the Federal Deposit Insurance Corporation (FDIC) up to $40,000. The one drawback you will find is that banks generally offer low interest rates on savings.

Savings and Loan Associations Most savings and loan associations do not offer checking accounts to customers. They specialize in savings accounts and loans, specifically home loans. As a specialist, they offer higher rates of interest on savings than the bank. Savings and loan associations often offer a higher rate of interest on time certificates and certificates of deposit than does the bank, although many banks are now within sight of meeting these rates. Deposits in savings and loan associations are insured by the Federal Savings and Loan Insurance Corporation (FSLIC) for up to $40,000.

Credit Unions Becoming increasingly popular is the credit union that draws its members from some specific group, employees of a company, members of a club, residents in a community, or others. Credit unions provide low-interest loans to members and savings are designated as shares in the union. Rates of interest vary and some may exceed the interest paid at a bank but seldom exceed that paid by the savings and loan. One advantage to saving your money with a credit union is that it will facilitate your obtaining a low-interest loan should the need arise.

Types of Saving Plans

Banks and savings and loan associations generally offer the same types of saving accounts, although they may call them by different names. The credit union, on the other hand, may offer only the regular savings account.

Regular Savings Account The greatest asset of this account is its liquidity. When you need the money, you can get it by simply filling out a withdrawal slip. Rates tend to be lowest on this type of account and if you withdraw prior to the payment of interest, you may lose the interest for that quarter completely. Also, if you make excessive withdrawals (most allow three per quarter), then there is the possibility that you will be asked to pay a service charge (ranging from $.25 to $1.00).

Regular savings accounts are a good way to start your savings. Banks will transfer money from your checking to your savings if you desire and you can make any deposit, no matter how small, to the account. Interest is earned from the day of deposit and is paid four times a year. Most banks and savings and loan associations will pay interest from the 1st of the month on money deposited by the 10th of the month. In order to receive interest, you must have a balance of at least $100 in your account. The only exception to this rule is the trust account for a minor child which receives interest no matter what the balance.

Christmas Club Accounts Savings accounts set up for the specific purpose of supplying you with money at the Christmas season. Interest on this account is the same as on a regular savings account. Its one advantage is that you receive a check about November 15, just in time to beat the Christmas rush. Christmas Club accounts can be closed out before the year ends but it is more involved than withdrawing from a regular savings account and, therefore, most people do not close these accounts. If you default on a Christmas Club payment, you are penalized only to the extent of losing the interest on the account. Whatever money you have already put into the account will still be returned to you on November 15.

There are two ways to open a Christmas Club account. You can either elect to have a certain amount deducted from your checking account each month or you can obtain a coupon book. A coupon book contains twenty-five coded coupons (the denomination of each designated by you according to how much you want to save). Payments are made every two weeks. Automatic deductions from checking accounts are usually made once a month. Christmas Club accounts are opened between November 1 and January 31 each year with October 31 being the last entry date. When signing up, you designate how much you want to save and at the end of the fifty-week period, you receive that amount in check form if you have made all the payments as agreed.

Time Deposits The one main difference between a time deposit and a regular savings account is that the time deposit is committed to savings for a certain period of time. Say, you take a time deposit for ninety days. That means that you cannot withdraw the money for ninety days. If you do, you are penalized by having to forfeit any or all of the interest you may have earned.

Interest rates on these types of accounts are higher than the regular savings. They, generally, come in two different types: (1) Certificates of Deposit, and (2) Investors Passbook Accounts.

Certificates of Deposit When you put your money into a certificate of deposit, you agree to leave it untouched for a period of time (or a *fixed-term*). This time period can range from thirty days to ten years, depending on how long you designate. You cannot add additional money to a certificate of deposit. It is for a fixed amount. If you wish to save additional amounts in this manner, you must purchase more certificates. You do not receive a passbook but rather a certificate that indicates the amount of money, the interest rate and the maturity date. Certificates of deposit are issued for nothing less than $500 for a maturity date of thirty days to four years; above four years, a minimum deposit of $1000 is required. Interest is usually not paid until the certificates mature. Early withdrawals are subject to substantial interest penalties. Rates of interest vary according to the amount of money invested and the time length of the certificate, as well as the economic conditions of the country at the time the certificate is purchased. Interest rates, however, tend to be considerably higher than the conventional savings account and if you do not plan to use your savings for a period of time, this an excellent saving method.

Investors Passbook Accounts This type of fixed-term savings vehicle provides some of the advantages of the regular savings account and some of the Certificate of Deposit. Like Certificates of Deposit, they pay higher interest rates and have specified maturity dates. Their similarity to savings accounts is that you receive a passbook and you can make additional deposits at any time.

There are three types of accounts in this savings plan, each dealing with the maturity period you choose—the three-month plan, the twelve-month plan, and the thirty-month plan. The amount of interest increases with the increase of the term of the investment. Initial deposit in this type of account must be at least $500. You can make additional deposits at any time in increments of at least $100.

Strict rules are imposed on this type of investors fixed-term account, namely:

1. At the maturity period, if the money is not withdrawn within ten days of the maturity date, it is reinvested for a term exactly the same as the first. In other words, if you invest $500 for three months and do not withdraw the funds at the end of three months or ten days thereafter, your money becomes reinvested for an additional three months.

2. Interest is credited to the account and any interest not withdrawn within ten days of the maturity date, becomes a part of the

principal and cannot be withdrawn until the account matures again.
    3. Additional deposits may be made to the account at any time.
Each deposit becomes a part of the total savings but bears a different
maturity date according to when it was deposited. For example, if
you deposit $500 on January 1 in a three-month account, that $500
will be mature on March 31. If, however, you deposit an additional
$500 on January 2, that will not mature until June 30. Rules are very
strict regarding the quarter sequences. If the maturity date is three
months, then the deposit must be in the account for three months, to
the *day*, and counting from the first of the month.

The passbook you are provided with will assist you in keeping
track of the money you have in the account and you will receive
a quarterly statement that will keep you informed about how
much money you have available for withdrawal. While earning
high interest rates, this account can be annoying if you do not
stay on top of it. If you miss a maturity date and your money is
reinvested, it can cause a problem if you had planned to withdraw. And as with all fixed-term accounts, there are strict penalties for early withdrawal.

Some Things You Should Know About Savings

Compound Interest—Before you put your money into a savings
account that appears to have a higher interest rate than another,
check out the method in which the interest is paid. Compound
interest means that interest is paid on the balance, not just the
principal. Thus, you earn interest on your interest if you do not
withdraw it. This type of interest payment can add up to considerably more than just a straight annual interest rate.

   Taxes—Any interest earned on a savings account over $10
must be reported on your income tax form. Each year you will
receive a form from the savings institution for filing with your
income tax.

   Frozen Accounts—Accounts that do not allow withdrawals.
Some of these do exist and you should make certain you can
afford to leave your money untouched for the period of time
designated before committing yourself.

   Interest Computed Daily—Your money earns interest from
the day you deposit until the day you withdraw.

   Maturity—The date that an agreement comes to an end.

New Places to Save Your Money

Women are becoming more and more aware of the need for financial independence, a need to direct their own course in life. Toward that end, women have banded together to form Women's Banks and Feminist Credit Unions. When you look for a savings institution, you might consider putting your money into those organizations specifically designed to help women not only save but invest and borrow.

Women's Banks—There are (1975) only two women's banks in the United States—The First Women's Bank in New York City and the Western Women's Bank in San Francisco. Both banks do not promise women special treatment regarding loans or savings but they do promise an understanding ear. Women's banks are scheduled to open in Los Angeles, California; San Diego, California; Greenwich, Connecticut; Washington, D. C.; Chicago, Illinois; Seattle, Washington; and Boston, Massachusetts.

Feminist Credit Unions—Early in 1976 there were nineteen feminist credit unions in the U.S. with three more in the planning stages. These credit unions are feminist-run, nonprofit savings and loan cooperatives that offer low-cost loans and savings accounts to members. They are chartered by the federal government and all deposits are insured as with any other credit union. Like the women's banks, the feminist credit union does not promise special treatment for women. However, most do offer solutions to credit problems. In some cases, loans are made to women who could not get a loan anywhere else. Feminist credit unions stress character rather than collateral. They are more concerned about your ability to repay the loan than your sex or marital status.

Savings at a Feminist Credit Union can earn interest as high as 7 percent, more even than most banks. Check out your local branch before you put your money elsewhere. According to the July, 1976 *Ms.* Magazine:

> The Greater New York Feminist Federal Credit Union opened last fall in Manhattan, and this union and some dozen others across the country have been loosely structured into the Feminist Economic Network. . . . the goals of the network include encouraging feminist credit unions in every state, and the practical sharing of

knowledge and experience to help newly organizing unions deal with specific problems. More broadly, the network hopes to develop strategies for feminist solutions to women's economic problems. For information; contact the Feminist Economic Network, P.O. Box 20008, Detroit, Michigan 48220.

Resources–Feminist Credit Unions

Bay Area Feminist FCU
944 Market Street, Room 617
San Francisco, CA 94102
(415) 391-3003

California Feminist FCU
P. O. Box 2329
San Diego, CA 92112
(714) 238-1922

Chicago Women's FCU
P. O. Box 163
Chicago, IL 60659
(312) 674-5650

Colorado Feminist Credit Union
1458 Pennsylvania Street
Denver, CO
(303) 837-0622

Connecticut Feminist FCU
170 York Street
New Haven, CT 06510
(203) 777-6330

Feminist FCU
P. O. Box 20008
Detroit, MI 48220
(313) 892-7190

Feminist FCU
Ann Arbor Branch
225 E. Liberty St., Rm. 203
Ann Arbor, MI 48104
(313) 662-5400

Feminist FCU
Lansing Branch
217 Townsend Street
Lansing, MI 48933
(517) 489-4521

First Pennsylvania Feminist CU
4th and Walnut Street
Harrisburg, PA 17101
(171) 761-1836

Florida Feminist Credit Union
7220 S.W. 61st Court
Miami, FL 33143
(305) 666-9804

Freedom Feminist FCU
P. O. Box 8123
Pittsburgh, PA 15217
(412) 521-5183

Houston Area Feminist FCU
2418 Travis
Houston, TX 77006
527-9108

Los Angeles Feminist FCU
1434 Westwood Blvd., Suite 4
Los Angeles, CA 90024
(213) 475-3889

Massachusetts Feminist FCU
186½ Hampshire Street
Cambridge, MA 02139
(617) 661-0450

Metro Toronto Women's CU
112 Spruce Street
Toronto, Ontario, Canada

New York Feminist FCU
23 Cornelia Street
New York, NY 10014
(212) 255-4664

Washington Area Feminist FCU
1424 16th St., N.W.
Washington, DC 20036
(202) 332-1132

Washington State Feminist FCU
Box 22382
Seattle, WA 98122
325-7162

Women's Southwest FCU
P. O. Box 431
Dallas, TX 75221
(214) 522-3560

Organizing

Saundra Daddio
3515 Fremont Avenue South
Minneapolis, MN 55408
(612) 822-4637

Feminist Federal CU (branch)
811 Cherry Street, #201
Columbia, MO 65201
(314) 449-2688

Caroline Sparks & Bat-Ami Bar On
135 E. Woodruff Avenue
Columbus, OH 43201
(614) 291-7543

5

Security–Insurance

Savings are a vital part of financial security but perhaps even more important than savings is insurance. Whatever sum of money you manage to store away in your savings, chances are it will not be great enough to cover medical bills should you be in a massive automobile accident, not to mention the damage to the car. Fire could destroy your home and furniture. Thieves could cart away all your valuable belongings. What then—could you afford to refurnish? A friend could slip on your kitchen floor and break a leg. Could you pay the medical costs? Could you afford to be sued for, say, $100,000?

If you can answer yes to any of these questions, then you are indeed a rare individual—the average person could not answer yes to even one. Thus, insurance. It is protection against what might happen but you hope will not. The insurance company bets that it will not happen to you. If you opt to buy insurance, then you are hedging against the possibility that it will.

There are all kinds of insurance. Film stars have been known to insure that part of their anatomy that has made them famous, their legs, bust or face. These types of policies are short-lived, usually obtained for their publicity value only. They do demonstrate, however, that you can insure just about "anything."

For the majority of us, though, automobile, homeowner's, renter's, life, health, burial, disability and fire insurance are more than ample to meet our needs. Chances are that you will not even need all of these. The idea is to explore them all, know what is available, assess your own needs and then decide.

Life Insurance

Life insurance is a "must," especially if you are the head of the household. No one can guarantee that you will live long enough to raise your children or pay off the house note or even pay all your bills. If you should die with no life insurance and little money in the bank, your relatives may not even have enough money to pay your funeral expenses. Buy life insurance because you are concerned for your children, your husband, your relatives or a close friend. You might think of life insurance as a final housecleaning, a chance to pay your bills and provide for your loved ones after you are gone.

Life insurance basically comes in two varieties, the kind that pays only on death and the one that can be converted to cash before death. There are variations on these predicated on when you pay the premiums, how much you pay and other factors. The kinds we explore here include: (1) straight life, (2) limited payment life, (3) endowment life, (4) modified life, and (5) term life.

Straight Life This type of life insurance policy is more than insurance on your life; it is an investment. It can be converted to cash whenever you desire, or you can elect to have monthly checks sent to you when you retire, or you can borrow against the cash you have invested in it. In short, whatever money you put into it you can get back. Note, however, that the cash value of this policy is only as great as the amount of money you have invested in it. You cannot collect any more than that amount unless you die. Premiums on straight life do not change over the years. What you are paying monthly at twenty, you will be paying at sixty-five.

With a straight life policy, you receive protection for a lifetime. There is no need to renew. If you should wish to cancel, you can do so, electing to take your investment in cash or taking monthly payments over an extended period of time. If you stop paying premiums, you may continue to receive coverage at a reduced amount of the face value of the policy ($15,000 instead of $25,000, for example) or elect to continue full coverage for a limited period of time.

Straight life insurance is a plus no matter how you look at it. You are guaranteed a cash return, before or after death. If you live beyond the age of retirement and wish, you can convert it into a nice retirement nestegg.

Limited Payment Life A variation of straight life, this policy differs in the method of paying the premiums. You agree to pay the premiums off in a specified time period, say over a ten-year period. Naturally, the premiums will be much higher than they would be if they were stretched out over three times that period, as the normal policy is. The overall cost of the policy, however, is not any higher and, in some cases, it may be lower since you are paying it off faster. This type of policy is designed for those who have a high income during a period of time in their life with the likelihood that the high income will not continue indefinitely. For example, the star baseball player, novelist or TV newscaster. Like the straight life policy, this one is convertible into cash.

Endowment Life   This type of policy is designed specifically with the cash value of the policy in mind. It is considered more of a savings than a life insurance policy. For example, you decide that you need $10,000 to put your child through college and you need the money in fifteen years. This policy will set the size of the premiums to reach this goal. Interest on your money will be low, usually 4 percent, but you will be amassing money for a specific purpose. For those who find it difficult to save, this policy is the answer.

Of course, should you die before the policy matures, your survivors collect the full value of the policy. You are assured that the money will be there for whatever reason you have designated, whether you live or die.

Modified Life   This type of policy is a variation of the straight life or the term life policy. Premiums are lower at the beginning of the policy and increase slightly over a period of years, eventually stabilizing. The idea behind this policy is that the earning power of the individual will be less when she is young and will increase as she gets older. Thus, she will be able to afford the policy if the premiums graduate with her salary increases.

Term Life   Term life has no cash value prior to death. Premiums are far lower than those policies that do have a cash value. There are variations on the term policy which enable you to convert to other types of insurance. Some forms of term life are renewable after a designated period of time; some continue for a lifetime. For one who desires only life insurance and has no interest in saving money through the policy, the low-cost term life is the one to choose.

Some Variations of Life Insurance

Decreasing Term. It is usually purchased to cover the cost of a home. It features a level premium with the cash value of the policy dropping each year, much as your mortgage does. Most who elect to take this type of insurance make certain the value of the policy coincides with the existing mortgage on the home. Then, if the insured dies, the home is paid in full. Some lending institutions require this policy for all mortgage loans. Decreasing term does not have to be used for mortgages, however; it can also be used to insure other long-range notes.

Family Plan Insurance. Some policies will insure the entire family. Usually, the amount of insurance on each member decreases with their considered importance in terms of money-making capabilities, i.e., head of household first with children insured for less. Amounts tend to be negligible, enough only to cover burial expenses.

Double Indemnity Life. The addition of a clause on your policy and a small added amount of money will provide twice the face value of the policy should the insured die accidentally.

Waiver of Premiums. Should you become disabled or financially unable to pay the premiums, you can cease payments for a time without losing the policy if you have added a "waiver of premiums" clause. This waiver must be requested when the policy is taken out and it will cost you a small additional sum of money.

Group Life. Your company or a group you are a member of may have a group life insurance policy that will meet your needs. Most group policies carry reduced premiums, some as much as 40 percent lower than what it would cost you to buy it alone. If you have access to such a policy, check it out first. Most employers provide such a policy, many at no cost to you.

Medical Insurance

If you ever plan to read the small print of an insurance policy, and you always should, read every word of it on your medical policy *before* you buy. There are too many medical policies on the market that promise the world but in actuality give you less than nothing. Promises like full coverage of all hospital bills, with the small print revealing that this coverage extends only to a specified time limit. Or the small print may reveal that it covers costs only up to a certain amount. Too often people sign up for medical insurance only to discover when it is too late that their "super" insurance is nothing more than a small flash on the total cost of the bill. It may cover anesthesia but not the anesthesiologist (his price is much greater than the drug); the hospital accommodations, if you are in a ward but not if you need intensive care in a private room. It may cover surgery, if you have a big toe removed but not if you have a hernia operation. Don't laugh. Medical policies tend to get very technical, some going so far as to outline in detail what the policy covers and how much it will pay on specific medical problems. They may name such things as dismemberment, paying, say, $1000 if you have an arm removed by surgery, or paying $500 for a broken leg.

Many of these policies that name specific amounts mean exactly that. They will pay only that amount on the ailment, no matter that you must pay the doctor, the hospital, emergency care and ambulance. You get only one lump sum from the insurance company.

Do not assume from this discourse that all medical policies are bad. They are not. In fact, they are a necessity, a positive one. If you do not have one, you are gambling and you will probably lose. The odds are that you will be hospitalized for some reason during your lifetime and hospital costs (running well over $100 a day just for a bed) will ruin you if you do not have some type of insurance. The point is: there are good policies and there are bad. Know which you are getting before you pay.

There are essentially five different types of medical insurance policies: (1) doctor, (2) surgery, (3) hospital, (4) disability, (5) doctor, surgery and hospital after a certain amount is reached. You can buy insurance for doctor's bills only, hospital only or surgery only. However, it makes more sense to buy a general policy that covers all three up to a certain limit, say $10,000. Beyond that point, you buy a major medical plan that covers you up to, say, $250,000.

Policies do not generally cover all expenses, no matter how good they are. The patient is left with a certain percentage, usually 20 percent after a certain amount is reached. For example, your policy may cover the first $500 completely if you are in an accident. After that, it may cover only 80 percent. Or it may cover the first $500 with you covering the next $500 and it taking over again after that. Or you may have to cover the first $500 with the insurance picking up expenses after that.

As you can see, there are many different variations and unless you know exactly what you are buying, you may be in for an unpleasant surprise just when you are in the least need of it.

For an additional premium, you can include on your policy such things as pregnancy, psychiatry, orthodontics, dental and other medical problems. Some of these may be a part of your policy but you will not know unless you check. Many medical policies will allow you to include dependent children in the coverage for little or no additional expense. Another thing to consider.

If you have access to a group policy, then, like life insurance, that is your best bet. Most employers provide a medical plan, some of them very good and many which do not cost you anything. Many of these group policies also allow you to add additional coverage for a minimum amount of money should you desire to do so. And if you should leave the company, many policies can remain in effect with you picking up the premiums. Check out all the benefits afforded by a group policy first, then go from there.

If you are married, your husband probably has you on his policy at work. Even after you are divorced, if you so stipulate in the divorce settlement, you can remain a part of that policy. This makes it much simpler for the newly independent woman who does not have the energy to seek out a good policy (she is too involved in getting her feet on the ground) and often does not have the money to buy one.

Disability Insurance

Should you become disabled you will become eligible for social security benefits after a certain period of time, provided you have been employed and been a paying member of the social security plan. Also many states provide disability insurance. Much like social security, premiums are deducted from your paycheck. Should you be disabled, you will receive a modest but welcome check from the state monthly. You must file for this. Many employers provide either disability or sick leave for employees injured on or off the job. This type of employee coverage may be included as part of the group medical policy.

All of these may provide enough income. However, if they do not, then you can purchase additional disability insurance for a modest sum. For example, $100 a week for a period not to exceed two years may cost you $125 a year in premiums—not much when you consider the return. However, this type of coverage can run into money over a period of years if you never use it. The secret is to check out the other sources available to you at no cost before you invest in additional coverage. Chances are you will not need additional coverage.

Automobile Insurance

Becoming increasingly available and, hopefully, soon to be nationwide is no-fault automobile insurance. This insurance assumes that the accident is no one's fault. Every insured victim collects for medical bills, unpaid wages and other losses. It releases all parties from the burden of proving who was at fault and protects an insured victim should the collision occur with an uninsured auto. If you do not have no-fault automobile insurance in your state, then you can choose from several different types of policies with many coverage plans, depending on how much you want to pay in premiums, how much coverage you feel you need and how much you use your automobile.

Liability   All states require that you carry a minimum amount of liability insurance on your automobile. It protects you against claims made by victims of an accident or any damaged property as a result of an accident caused by you.

Bodily Injury Liability. Usually a part of your liability policy, this covers bodily injury or death to victims in an accident caused by you or the person driving your car.

Uninsured Motorist. Even though the law requires it, some motorists do not carry insurance. If you should be hit by one of these and he is at fault, your insurance company will cover all your costs if you have an uninsured motorist rider on your policy.

Collision. If you should collide with another car, or an object, this type of insurance will cover the damage to your car whether you are to blame or not. Collision usually carries a deductible of approximately $100, meaning that you pay the first $100 of the repair bill.

Medical. This policy covers the medical expenses of you and any riders in your car, no matter who is at fault. It also covers you as a passenger in another car.

Comprehensive. In the event of fire, flood, theft, vandalism, lightning, explosions, falling objects and more, your car is protected by this policy. It does not include collision.

Combination. As it indicates, a combination of the benefits of medical, liability, accidental death and uninsured motorist protection in one policy.

Before You Buy Auto Insurance   Before you commit to a certain insurance policy, consider these things:

1.   How much is your car worth? Is the cost of the insurance excessive in terms of that value?

2.   Are you a nonsmoker? This may make you eligible for a discount.

3.   Do you already have health insurance? If so, does it cover you sufficiently should you have an automobile accident? Perhaps you can save additional money by eliminating yourself in the medical coverage of the auto policy.

4.   How far do you drive to work? Many policies charge premiums based on how much the car is driven on a daily basis.

5.   Have you one car already insured? A second car insured by a company will generally be insured for less than the first, say, a 20 percent discount.

6.   Does the policy include car rental while your car is being repaired after an accident? This expense could run into a large sum in a short period of time.

7.   Are you a nondrinker? Discounts may be available.

8.   If you are considering the purchase of a new car, inquire about the rates before you buy. The new, high-powered models require bigger insurance premiums.

Homeowner's Insurance

To protect your home against fire, theft and personal liability, you need to purchase a homeowner's policy. This type of policy comes in variations much the same as all other insurance policies. For example, for an additional premium, you can insure your home against earthquake or tidal waves or an exploding hot water heater. Whatever the eventuality, you can find an insurance to cover it if you feel you need it.

You should plan to insure your home for at least 80 percent of its value. If you are not sure of the value, contact the real estate agent who sold you the home or hire an appraiser (they charge about $25) to appraise the home for you. In the event of the destruction of your home, an insurance adjustor will make a determination of the value of the home based on appraisal and values in the neighborhood, and the settlement will be based on that figure. If, for example, you paid $30,000 for the home but over the years it has deteriorated and the neighborhood has deteriorated as well, it may be appraised at $20,000 not $30,000. There is nothing you can do about this eventuality, but you should be aware that it can happen.

The same type of depreciation holds true for any personal property you may have in the house. You are more likely to feel this type of depreciation than that on your home. Chances are you will at some time lose some personal item in your house by theft or fire or some other calamity. When you go to collect on your homeowner's policy, you will discover that the $1000 TV set you bought two years ago is now worth only $500. It is this type of depreciation that can really hit the pocketbook hard, especially if thieves clean out your house entirely.

Homeowner's also covers, as a general part of the policy, personal liability. That means, simply, that if someone visiting your home injures themselves, their medical expenses and any settlements will be covered. Since you are also liable for portions of your property accessible to the public (like the front yard), this coverage can be important. There have been cases where children have climbed over fences and drowned in backyard swimming pools and courts found the homeowner liable. There are a hundred eventualities that could hit you for personal liability, no matter how careful you are. If you own a home, then you must have homeowner's insurance. Include it in your monthly mortgage payments. It is a necessity that is well worth the expense.

Renter's Insurance

A renter's insurance policy is basically the same as the homeowner's with the exception that the living structure is not included. The policy insures personal property against fire and theft and you against personal liability. You can add additional coverage for an added premium. With the high incidence of theft in rental units, this type of policy is highly desirable, especially if you own your own furniture and other valuables, such as television, stereo, paintings or antiques.

Burial Insurance

Burial insurance is basically the same as term life insurance, with the exception that it is generally for a very small sum, say, $2000. Premiums are very low and there is no cash value. Simply, you are setting money aside to pay for your funeral expenses, nothing more. It is payable only on death.

Conclusion

All the insurance available to you is not listed here. Nor is each one that is listed here explored in depth. Those listed, however, are considered to be the most important and those which you should strongly think of purchasing. Use the information in this chapter only as a guide to start you on the road toward insurance security.

6

Investing–The Stock Market

There is a difference between saving your money and investing it. Generally, if you are saving your money, you have it tucked away somewhere where you know it is safe. It is guaranteed by the government and it will be there when you want it. You may be earning interest at the rate of 5, 6, or even 7 percent, maybe more.

If you choose to invest your money, however, you are putting it on the line. You are exercising a belief in a product, a person or a business. There are no assurances; there is no certainty that you will get your money back. There is no interest rate. You are taking a risk, a risk that may reap you large or small profits or leave you with less than you started. It could even wipe out all you've invested.

One of the most popular ways to invest money is through stock. Some 30,900,000 Americans were shareholders in 1974, and another 100 million were indirect owners through savings accounts, insurance companies, pension funds and other financial institutions that invested in stocks. Stocks have been an American way of life since America began. In 1789 Congress authorized the issue of $80,000,000 in stock to help pay for the cost of the Revolutionary War. Since there was no organized way of buying or selling the stock, people were reluctant to invest. In 1792, a group of men rallied to the situation and set up what was to be the beginning of the New York Stock Exchange under a buttonweed tree only a few blocks from the present site of the Stock Exchange. Today, the New York Stock Exchange is the recognized leader in the stock market.

To own stock it is generally thought that you must be rich or at least have a great deal of cash on hand. This is not so. As a matter of fact, almost the opposite is true. A New York Stock Exchange survey revealed that more than half of all shareholders

48

reported annual family income of less than $15,000 and half of all portfolios (a shareholder's summary or "bible" of his investments) have a current market value of less than $10,000.

It was once thought you needed at least $5000 to invest in stocks. Some brokerage firms will still not accept you if you plan to start your portfolio with less, but these are fast declining. Today you need only a desire to invest. You can work out the details, depending on your income and the way you wish to invest. Anyone can be a stockholder today, even a woman with little income at present. With wise planning and a complete knowledge of the market, it is possible to come out with a sizable amount of money.

Banking your money can yield you only a limited amount of return on your money. Depending on what type of account you put it into, you can earn from 4 to 8 percent interest, but there is no growth possible in the *original* amount you have invested. The stock market, on the other hand, can increase your money by as much as 100 or even 500 percent over a period of years. The average stock gain in a year is a little over 9 percent, not astronomical but more than a bank would yield. Of course, nothing says that your stock will rise in value. It may decline. If it does, then you lose money. That's where the risk is involved. You stand to gain more by investing in stocks but you also stand to lose. It is a reality that you must live with if you decide to invest in the stock market. Even though there is a certain amount of risk involved, investing in stock is not the same as going to Reno and putting your money down on the dice table. In Reno you depend totally on luck. In the stock market, you depend on the shrewd business sense of either yourself or a professional broker hired to handle your portfolio. Making it in the stock market is possible—if you know how it works (and you have a little luck).

What Are Stocks?

Stocks are part ownership in a business. If, for example, you own 130 shares of General Motors and General Motors has 1,300,000 shares outstanding then you own 1/10,000 interest in General Motors. You actually own part of the business and, depending on the type of stock you hold, you have a proportionate say in the policies of the company. If the company suffers reverses, then you stand to lose a portion or all of your money. If the company grows, then you can expect to increase your money. The growth or decline of the company will be reflected in the price of the stock. If you buy at $58 a share and the stock drops to $45 a share, you lose $13 a share. If you, however, keep the stock and ride out the decline and the stock rises to $75 a share, then you increase your investment by $17 a share.

Some stocks offer dividends. This is simply a payment to the stockholders of a portion of the earnings of the company. Paid either quarterly or yearly, dividends on shares vary and may be as low as a few cents to several dollars a share, or more. Some dividends are fixed, say $1 or $2 a share, others fluctuate with the earnings. If earnings are low, there are some years when you may not receive any at all. Some stocks pour all their earnings back into the company and thus no dividends are distributed. These are generally called growth stocks (companies that are in the process of developing and need the added capital). Dividends may or may not be important to you, depending on how you wish to capitalize on your investment.

What Kinds of Stock?

Basically, there are two kinds of stock, preferred and common.

Preferred stock is given preferential treatment over the common stock. It generally has the following rights: (1) A claim to the fixed dividend prior to common stock. If, for example, the company cannot pay all the dividends, the preferred stockholder is paid first. The common stockholder receives his dividend if there are enough funds remaining. (2) A claim to the assets of the company should it go out of business. A preferred stockholder may receive a portion of his investment back while the common stockholder may receive little or nothing. Generally, preferred stockholders, while enjoying the above mentioned privileges, do not have a say in the company as does the common stockholder. They cannot vote. Also, the preferred stockholder can generally expect no more than the fixed dividend as outlined in the stock certificate, no matter how much the company may prosper. If the company goes into decline, the dividend may be omitted or reduced and unless the certificate states that the dividend is cumulative, the dividend may never be paid.

Common stock is the most popular of all stocks traded. Many companies have only one issue of stock—generally, common stock. If you own common stock, you own a part of the business. You buy a say in the company, proportionate to your investment. You can vote on policies, directors, etc. You may make suggestions to the board, offer ideas which the board may choose to handle or may call for a general vote of the shareholders. That is not to say that any idea you present will be acted upon, but you do have the option of conveying your feelings about the business and how it is being run.

If times are good, your dividends may be increased. If they are bad or if the company decides to reinvest in the company for expansion purposes or whatever, dividends may not be paid at all.

There are some 1500 common stocks listed on the New York Stock Exchange; over 30,000 listed on the over-the-counter market. Aside from preferred or common, stocks may be referred to in any number of other ways usually dependent on some special feature. They include the following:

Blue Chip Stock. Stocks that have proven themselves over the years. Usually from the larger, more affluent company that has recorded fairly good earnings and regular dividends, these stocks are generally considered "safe" buys. The returns will most likely not be much above what you would receive had you invested your money in a bank or bond but the returns can be considered relatively certain.

Cyclical Stock. Stocks that generally follow the trend of the specific business. For example, the firecracker industry enjoys a great deal of business on the Fourth of July while the toy industry may record its highest sales during the Christmas season. With this type of stock, the highs and lows are generally predictable.

Defensive Stock. Stocks that enjoy more stability during economic upheaval. You can depend on them to pay dividends and remain fairly stable in the market during a time when most stocks are falling to record lows.

Dollar Stock. Sometimes referred to as Penny Stocks, these are low priced stocks that are considered risky. Such stocks sell for $10 and under, many for less than a dollar. Since they cost so little, they are highly tempting to the new investor. The profits can be great if the stocks increase in value. However, you could lose everything if the stock fails. Considered very high risk.

Ex-Dividend Stock. This type of stock is so called due to the time and manner of its sale. If you buy an ex-dividend stock, it means simply that the shareholder is selling you the stock only and he retains the right to collect the next dividend. All dividends after that will, of course, be yours. A stock is sold ex-dividend not by choice but merely because the company involved has already prepared the necessary paper to pay the dividend to the previous owner.

Ex-Rights Stock. A company offers a shareholder the opportunity to buy new or additional stock, sometimes at a special rate. This is called a "right." If you buy stock designated ex-rights, you are buying only the stock put up for sale. The previous owner retains the rights.

Glamour Stock. A stock that is enjoying a new surge in price due to popularity over a new invention, process or product. These stocks are generally short-lived unless the glamour aspect can be counted on to continue and develop into a substantial base for the company.

Growth Stock. These stocks are considered one of the best places to increase your money rapidly or lose it just as rapidly. Growth stocks record a consistent rise, usually above that of the economy as a whole or of other stocks on the market. Generally, they do not pay dividends, preferring instead to reinvest the money in the company to spur even more growth. If growth stocks do go down, the decrease is usually small with a return to an even higher value. Obviously, this type of stock is the investor's dream, a dream that is not easily found.

Income Stock. This type of stock pays dividends regularly. The value of the stock, however, tends to be very little. Income stocks are for the investor who wishes to collect a yearly dividend check and is not particularly interested in a long-range plan of increasing her money. Income stock are another form of savings. You can be relatively sure that the stock will not fall below what you paid for it and you can expect a regular dividend check.

New Issue Stock. As the name indicates, this is a new issue of stock. It is considered high risk if it is a new company. If you wish to pursue this type of stock, it requires a great deal of homework on your part to be certain that your investment is relatively safe. As with most high risk situations, the rewards could be great but the losses likewise could be great. Your first order of business when considering the purchase of this type of stock is to obtain a copy of the prospectus of the company (a statement of what the company plans to do and what it feels are its chances of success). By law, a prospectus must be accurate and you will find many eye-opening statements in it which will either confirm or alleviate your fears.

Split Stock. When the company decides to *split* their stock, you usually get two stocks for one (occasionally three for one). For example, if you own 200 shares before a two-for-one split, you own 400 after. This does not increase the value of your share since the cost per share splits as well, i.e., if your 200 shares were worth $100 each, your 400 shares will be worth $50 each. However, a stock split generally drives up the price of a share. More investors are interested in purchasing the stock at a lower price. It is actually within the reach of more investors. Also, if the stock split is known about within the market before the actual split, it tends to drive the cost of a share up. A stock split is generally considered a plus for the shareholder.

What Is a Stock Exchange?

When most people think of stocks, they think of the New York Stock Exchange on Wall Street. Actually, the majority of stocks are not listed on the New York Stock Exchange. It has gained so much prestige because it lists the largest companies in the country and has been in operation the longest.

"Of all the companies in business today, less than 1 percent are listed on the New York Stock Exchange, but those listed represent most of the largest and most profitable companies in the United States.

"Almost 80 percent of these companies paid cash dividends in the last 12 months and some 700 have paid dividends every single quarter for 20 up to more than 100 years. They provide jobs for about one fifth of the United States labor force. These companies produce practically all the automobiles and trucks made in this country, more than 90 percent of all aluminum, copper and cement and operate 97 percent of the telephones in service. In a recent year, these companies paid over $18 billion in federal, state and foreign income taxes." (From the New York Stock Exchange's own publication, "Understanding the New York Stock Exchange.")

Basically, the reason so few companies belong to the New York Stock Exchange is due to the rigid requirements set forth. Aside from its criteria that the company be "a going concern with substantial assets and demonstrated earning power," the Exchange requires the following: (1) that it have an earning power of $2.5 million annually before taxes, (2) that it have a minimum of 1 million shares publicly held, with not less than 2000 round-lot shareholders, (3) that the publicly held common shares have a minimum market value of $16 million. Other regulations include the preparation of financial statements for all shareholders, the stipulation that all shareholders have the right to vote each share owned, and a transfer agent and registrant must be located in New York City.

Obviously, not everyone can qualify for the New York Stock Exchange. Working with the New York Stock Exchange are some 13 national exchanges in the United States:

The American Stock Exchange
The Boston Stock Exchange
The Chicago Board of Trade
The Cincinnati Stock Exchange
The Detroit Stock Exchange
The Midwest Stock Exchange
The National Stock Exchange
The Pacific Stock Exchange
The Philadelphia-Baltimore-Washington Stock Exchange
The Pittsburgh Stock Exchange
The Salt Lake Stock Exchange
The Spokane Stock Exchange

To understand how they operate let's look at the New York Stock Exchange.

The New York Stock Exchange is, as its title designates, a place where stock is exchanged. It is a nonprofit organization where member stock brokers may buy and sell. Membership in the exchange is limited and presently totals 1366, representing some 500 partnerships or corporations. A stockbroker cannot just walk into the stock exchange and begin trading. He must buy a seat. The price of seat has ranged in recent years from $38,000 to $515,000. In addition, there is an initiation fee of $7500 and annual dues of $1500. Being a member of the stock exchange is not an easy or inexpensive matter. If you can find a brokerage house that is a member, then you can be assured that the brokerage firm has the assets and esteem in the investment community to warrant your confidence.

What happens on the stock exchange floor is relatively simple. Say you want to buy 20 shares of American Telephone and Telegraph (the most widely owned company listed on the exchange, having some 3,000,000 shareholders). You telephone your broker (an agent hired by you to purchase the necessary stock) and direct him to buy 20 shares of AT&T. He in turn phones or teletypes his man on the floor of the exchange who goes to the location of that stock on the floor (each stock is designated a certain trading spot). He discovers that the asking price is $50 per share. Depending on your directions (you may have told him to buy at the asking price or designated that you did not wish to pay more than $49 a share), he will either buy at the asking price or offer the lower price and see if there are any takers. The person he is dealing with represents someone else who owns 20 shares of AT&T and wants to sell. Your agent and the other agent must come to terms agreeable to both you and the seller to consummate the deal.

So, the New York Stock Exchange or any other exchange does not actually do the buying and selling. It only provides a place for the transaction and records and transmits the result via ticker tape to all its member brokers across the country. In this way, stocks rise and fall. If the demand is high, then you can ask for and get more for a stock. If the demand is low, then you must sell short (below what you initially paid), if you can indeed find a buyer at all.

If the Stock Is Not Listed on the Exchange

What of the 99 percent of American companies that cannot qualify for the New York Stock Exchange? Where do you buy their stock?

Some are listed as regional stock in the areas where the company is located but most are traded *over-the-counter*. This term refers to a system of stockbrokers who, through a system of sophisticated communications, buy and sell stock that does not qualify for the Stock Exchange. This over-the-counter market dwarfs in number those stocks carried on all the exchanges put together and yet all trading is done personally by your broker. There is, generally, no middle man.

Most brokers do over-the-counter buying and selling on the NASDAQ system, a system of computers that record all offers to buy and sell. In this way, the broker is aware of the current selling price of the stock and can regulate his transaction accordingly. This computer, however, is used only as a reference; the actual transaction is done over the telephone from one broker to another.

Stocks traded over-the-counter are usually those of smaller companies. Many are classified as *growth* stocks—shares in firms that have not yet proven themselves but that have a great deal of potential. There are exceptions—some very large, well estalished companies such as American Express are still traded over-the-counter.

Should You Buy an Option?

Another type of trading takes place at the Chicago Board and Options Exchange. It caters to the *option* buyer. Unless you have been involved in the stock market in some way, you most likely will have had no contact with this practice. Quite simply, it is buying an option on a stock purchase or a stock sell. In other words, if you feel that a certain stock is going to rise in price but you do not have the inclination or the money to buy the shares, you may buy an option or, as it is generally referred to, *a call*. For, say, $500 you may buy a "call" on 200 shares of AT&T at $70 a share for a six-month period. If the stock goes up during that period of time, you can exercise your "call" and buy the stock. You then turn around and sell the stock at the higher market price, making a nice profit. Deducting the price of your option and the brokerage commission fees, your profit could still be substantial. The opposite of a call is a *put*. This means that you buy an option to sell. It works the same way as a call.

Buying a put or a call does not guarantee you success, but it does lower your investment and, should the stock fail, it might considerably lower your loss. For example, if the aforementioned stock had fallen to $40 a share and you bought at $70 a share, you would have lost $6000. By buying an option instead, you would lose only the price of the option, $500. If you choose not to exercise the option, you merely let it expire and lose the money you paid for it.

The Chicago Board and Options Exchange was opened in 1973, specifically to handle put and call options. It is the only exchange of its kind in the country. Options are available from some twenty dealers who are members of the Put and Call Brokers Association. Many of these advertise in newspapers. You can deal through them or through your own broker; most brokerage houses have departments specifically set up for put and call options.

How to Buy Stock

Exercising an option is only one way to buy or sell stock. There are others, many of which are so complicated that it is best not to confuse those of us who are beginners with the varieties. Trying to explain these variations is a job only the experienced broker should tackle.

Some ways of buying stock which the beginner should understand include the following:

Round Lot—an accepted unit of trading in stocks, usually in lots of 100 shares.

Odd Lot—the purchase or sale of stock below the round lot designation. Many brokers will not handle accounts that deal in odd lots. On the Stock Exchange floor, there are special odd-lot dealers who handle such transactions. An odd lot may consist of from 1 to 99 shares in active stock.

Margin Buying—purchasing stock basically on the credit of your broker with only partial capital put up by you. The Federal Reserve Board designates the margin permitted on all stock on the exchange. For example, if you wish to purchase stock valued at $5000 and the Federal Reserve Board has set the margin at 50 percent, then you must put up 50 percent of the purchase price. The broker is allowed to advance the remainder. The advantage of doing this is obvious. You do not have to invest the total capital and yet the stock belongs to you. However, if the stock should fall to a value of $4000, then you would receive what is termed a *margin call* from your broker. The margin call is a request for additional funds to cover the margin set by the Federal Reserve Board. In this example, with the margin at 50 percent, you owe your broker $2500. If the stock should fall to $4000, the $2500 you owe your broker is not within the 50 percent margin which is now $2000. You must, therefore, cover the margin with an additional $500. Margin buying does not protect you from loss or guarantee you gains. It is simply another way to invest when you do not have all the necessary capital or when you choose not to tie up the money required for a specific transaction.

Selling Short—selling short is the opposite of the usual stock market rule. It is predicated on the hope that the stock will drop in value. What happens is this. The price of the stock may be at $40 a share. You sell 100 shares through your broker. You actually do have 100 shares of this stock but through a prearranged agreement with your broker, you borrow the necessary shares from him. Now you wait, hoping that the stock will drop. Say it does. It is now selling at $30 a share. You buy 100 shares for $3000 and repay the 100 shares you borrowed from your broker. Thus, you have sold at $40 a share pocketing $4000, used $3000 of that to reimburse your broker, and walked away with a $1000 profit, less brokerage fees. Not a bad investment.

It, however, does not always work that way. Say the stock soars to $60 a share. The time limit on the deal with your broker comes to an end and you are forced to buy at $60, making your investment $6000. You only made $4000 on the short selling deal and thus you stand to lose $2000 plus your brokerage fee. Short selling, like puts and calls, is best left to the experienced investor. Otherwise, you might find yourself on the heavy side of a losing proposition.

Limit Order—placing an order to buy or sell at a price no lower than that designated. For example, you may put up 100 shares with a limit order of $35. That means simply that your broker has your authorization to sell at not below $35. If the stock drops below that and does not rise, then the sell is not made.

Stop Order—this is used as a means of protecting a paper profit (a profit that you have not yet realized since you have not sold the stock). Say you bought at $30 a share and it now sells for $50 a share. The $20 per share profit is a paper profit until you actually sell the stock. Stop Orders are used as a means of limiting a loss, too. For example, you may enter a stop order to sell at $30 stocks which you initially paid $35 a share for. If the stock should begin falling and reach the $30 level, then the broker, without contacting you, will sell. In the profit direction, you may enter a stop order to sell the same stock at $50. If the value rises to $50, the broker will sell, thus protecting the profit. Both are used as a hedge against loss, whether it be a loss of part of the initial investment or a loss of paper profit. Stop orders may be initiated for one day, one week, a month or more. If the order is not acted on in the designated time, it expires.

GTC Orders—if an investor wants a stop order or a limit order to hold indefinitely, he gives his broker a GTC order (a good-till-cancelled order). It is carried by the broker as an open order until it is either acted on or cancelled.

Warrant—an offer to an investor that enables him to buy a certain number of shares at a specified price. The warrant may be offered to investors not now shareholders as an inducement to buy. It is similar to a right but usually has a longer life. Some are issued for a specific time limit; others never expire.

Rights—when new shares of stock are issued, the value of the stock already in existence may be reduced proportionately, especially if it is a stock split. In order to assist the shareholder in retaining her investment in the company, rights may be offered. Rights are an opportunity for the shareholder to purchase the necessary stocks, at a reduced price, in order to keep her percentage of ownership in the company. Say you own 20 shares in the company, you may be offered a right to buy additional shares to retain the percentage of ownership you now enjoy. You may either exercise the right and buy the additional shares or you may sell the right. Rights are always easy to sell since the price of the stock offered in a right is generally far below the actual market value.

Should You Have a Broker?

For the beginner, buying stocks through a broker is the best bet—if you can find one who will take a small investor. A broker is a trained expert. She knows all the jargon of the investment world and all the tricks. She can help you develop a portfolio that best reflects your needs, whether you are interested in dividends or long-range gains. A stockbroker also knows what stocks are most likely to make money. There is no guarantee that she will make the right decision, but she certainly has more expertise on the subject than the average investor. Once you have developed a knowledge of the market, you might wish to try your own system but, initially, it is wise to trust a broker.

Your first rule with your broker should be, above all, to tell the truth. Don't try to pretend you can afford to lose money when you cannot. Don't try to pretend that you can afford to invest more than you actually can. She will find out soon enough what the truth is and the finding out may be disastrous for you if you don't level with her from the beginning.

Choosing a Broker   Who you choose for your broker should be of the highest priority. For those with only a small amount to invest it may be difficult to find one. If you have a friend or business acquaintance who can recommend someone to you, and vice versa, that is the best possible way.

If you don't know of anyone, then you may send for a pamphlet, free of charge, which lists hundreds of members of the New York Stock Exchange who are willing to accept small accounts (since as a beginner your account is likely to be small, initially). Send to: Small Account Directory, New York Stock Exchange, P. O. Box 1971, Radio City Station, N.Y., NY 10019. The directory not only lists brokers all over the U.S. but gives a brief outline of what type of accounts they are willing to handle. But be careful and try to be as well informed as possible; there are unscrupulous stock brokers. You should have every confidence in yours since they will be handling your savings.

Securities Investor Protection Act   For your protection, and as a result of the fall of the stock market in the late 1960s, the Securities Investor Protection Act was put on the books in 1970. What the act does is offer the investor the same protection at the brokerage that you enjoy in banking through the FDIC. If you are investing any money at all, it is wise to do it with a brokerage firm that is a member of SIPC. What it means to you is that you are protected to the amount of $50,000 and even more if you split your account (putting one in your name, another in your husband's name and still another in a joint account). Each account is guaranteed up to $50,000. Unless you are a very heavy investor, that amount will more than cover you should the brokerage firm fail.

The SIPC does *not* protect you against loss in the stock market, only against loss through the brokerage firm. For example, you may have entrusted your stock to the firm, allowed them to keep their name on the stock certificates and handle the stock transactions totally with only your approval of their moves. In that case, or if you have given them a certain amount of money to buy stocks or in any number of other circumstances the SIPC will protect the money you have directly invested in the brokerage firm should the firm fail.

Investment Plans

In addition to trading with a stockbroker there are the following ways to invest. For information on how to set these up ask the manager of your bank, try the financial editor of your local paper, or ask your librarian for help.

Dollar Cost Averaging. A system whereby you invest a fixed amount regularly in a certain stock. There is a minimum amount and time period; you agree to invest at least a certain amount in a certain stock every quarter. (The fee is deducted automatically.) This is an excellent way to increase your portfolio but unless you watch the stock carefully and choose your purchase date (you are allowed a great deal of leeway on the exact date) to accomodate any price fluctuations, you could end up buying at just the time that the stock soars to a record high. One of the best known of these plans is Monthly Investment Plan (MIP). Most brokerage houses can get the address for you.

Brokerage House Investment Plans. A plan which enables you to invest a certain sum of money, say $5 or $5000 on a fairly regular basis. You are not obligated to remit a certain sum every month or even every quarter. Rather you decide when you can afford to invest the money. When you do send the brokerage firm the money, it buys a share or a portion of a share in your name in a stock designated by you. This is only one way of handling the plan. Other methods vary from one brokerage firm to the next.

Bank Plans. Some banks, not many yet, offer their depositors the option of an automatic checking or savings withdrawal at a predetermined time with the money invested in stocks. Because your money is invested along with other bank customers, you may receive a fraction of a share. At this point in time, this service is limited to the top twenty-five blue chip stocks selected by Standard & Poor's. You, of course, choose the stock you wish your money invested in. A plus to this arrangement is that banks generally charge low commission rates. A disadvantage is that banks generally do not buy according to the rise and fall of the market. They buy on a certain day. If the stock happens to be at an all-time high that day, then you buy at a high and stand to lose.

Employer Investment Plans. By far the most beneficial and easiest way for the new investor to "get his feet wet" in the stock market is through an Employer Investment Plan. Generally, these plans offer the employee the right to buy certain shares in the company (the one you are working for) at a reduced rate. Some companies may even offer one free share for each one purchased. This is the safest way to invest. You have direct knowledge of the company. You have a good idea of whether it is a good risk.

Dividend Reinvesting. As the name implies, dividend reinvesting is authorizing the reinvestment of any dividend money in additional stock. Since dividends rarely add up to enough to purchase a full share of stock, these dealings are usually made through a bank. For example, your dividend check, along with others, is sent to the bank on your request. The bank then uses that dividend to buy you a share or a fraction of a share. Even if the dividend is low, this is a sure way to slowly add to your holdings in a company.

Stockholder Purchase Plans. Some companies offer shareholders the opportunity to buy ten to a thousand shares of stock each month. The company handles the transaction, eliminating the need for a broker and thus eliminating his fee. You pay the company service fee which is far lower. The one disadvantage to this plan is that you have no control over when the stock is purchased. The resulting cost may be far above what you feel the stock should be selling for at that time.

Investment Clubs. One of the most popular ways to invest these days is through an investment club. The investment club is from ten to twenty investors (fifteen is considered a good number) who band together to pool their knowledge of the stock market and their money to make the greatest impact. Each member agrees to contribute a set amount of money each month. Later, once the club is moving, some members may decide to invest more. When you join an investment club, you actually buy shares of the club. The club, in turn, buys stock. Generally, in its early days, members agree not to touch any profits. They are plowed back into the club to buy even more stocks.

Anyone can form an investment club, even you. All you need is a number of women or men willing to invest and a broker who agrees to handle the club transactions. Finding a broker is the first order of business of the club. There are some brokers who will not handle an investment club, although more and more of them are realizing the potential commission benefit to them through association with a number of investment-minded people. The popularity of the investment club in the U.S. is clearly felt in the number now active, some 60,000 clubs and 200,000 members at last count. If you wish to start one, you can obtain information including stock selection guides and a portfolio management guide from The National Association of Investment Clubs, P. O. Box 220, Royal Oak, MI 48068.

Beginning a club requires formalizing investment procedures, drawing up a written agreement covering the club's investment policy, deciding which stocks to include in the initial portfolio, drawing up rules for members who wish to sell their shares, and bringing in new members. The fifty-page investment club manual from the The National Association of Investment Clubs will assist you in wading through all the initial details.

Investment clubs can be a boon to the new investor. It will allow her to start small (usually members agree to sums of $10 to $50 a month as the designated investment in the club). The club also allows you greater buying power (with the added money of your fellow members) on the market and thus your profits (and losses) will be proportionately higher. Generally, investment clubs have a good track record. The diversified backgrounds of the members seems to assure more astute judgment. If you do not wish to begin your own club, a local broker may be able to direct you to a club already in existence that for one reason or another has an opening.

Bears, Bulls and Other Stock Market Jargon You Should Know

If you have heard anything about the stock market, you have heard the terms *bull* or *bear* about the market or an investor. The two terms are as common to the market as *love* is to tennis. A bear market is a result of many people deciding at the same time to sell stock. The wide range of selling forces the stock price to decline substantially. If the price drop is prolonged, it is said to be a bear market. An extended bear market can cause panic selling thus causing the average price of stock to decline even further. (Continued decline can cause a *crash*.) A bull market is just the opposite. Many people decide to buy at the same time causing a resulting rise in the average price of a share of stock. An investor is bullish when he feels that the market will go up, bearish when he feels it will decline.

The language of Wall Street is varied and unless you have been on the street for an extended period of time, you most likely know very little of it. Even more likely is the possibility that you will learn only a fraction of it in your investment career. One dictionary of words used in the market includes some 1200 listings. There are few who could master a list like that. A few of the terms have already been defined. A few more of some importance follow.

Averages and Indexes—A measurement of stock market trends. These tend to be very broad and do not necessarily reflect the trend of a stock owned by you. For example, the trend may be downward while your stock value is rising.

The most commonly quoted average is the Dow Jones Average. It is the one you generally hear quoted on the late night news and flashed outside banks or brokerage houses. Dow Jones averages are based on a select number of blue chip stocks, some thirty. The stocks are chosen as a representative sample of the larger, more stable companies that reflect the American economy.

The Standard and Poor's Average, on the other hand, reflects 90 percent of the market value of all stock listed on the New York Stock Exchange. It includes 500 stocks divided in this manner—425 industrials, 25 railroads and 50 utilities.

Considered most representative of the market is the New York Stock Exchange Index. Other indexes include the American Stock Exchange Index, the National Quotation Bureau's Average and the

Associated Press Average. All reflect general tendencies of the market and not necessarily a particular stock.

Bid and Asked—The bid is the highest price offered for a stock during a transaction. The asked price is the lowest price offered to sell.

Big Board—A term given to the New York Stock Exchange and referring to its electronic board which lists more stocks than any other exchange.

Capital Gain or Capital Loss—When you sell stocks, you either make or lose money. Any money you make is capital gain; any you lose, capital loss. Gains and losses may be designated long term or short term, depending on the investment period, and taxed accordingly by the U.S. Government.

Commission—A fee charged by the broker to either buy or sell stocks, paid by the investor.

Convertible—A share of preferred stock which can be converted at some future time into shares of common stock, if you so desire.

Discretionary Account—An account in which an investor allows a broker to handle his stocks with little specific directions on a given transaction. In other words, if the broker sees a good buy or thinks he should sell to hedge the fall of the stock, he has your authority to do so without contacting you first.

Financial Statement—An annual, semiannual or quarterly report of a company's earnings, losses, taxes and expenses. All shareholders receive these reports and investors considering the purchase of the company stock use them to confirm or obviate their decision to buy.

Going Public—The process that a privately owned company may go through in order to place its shares on the market for public purchase.

Listed Stock—A stock that appears on the New York Stock Exchange or one of the other recognized exchanges. In order to be listed, the company must pass rigid standards laid down by the Securities and Exchange Commission.

Market Price—The price at which a stock is selling on the market at a given time.

Paper Profit—A profit you may have "on paper" but have not yet cashed. A paper loss is just the opposite.

Portfolio—The accumulated stocks held by an investor at a given period.

Price/Earnings Ratio—The ratio between the current selling price of the stock and its annual earnings per share. This can be calculated by dividing the stock price by the earnings.

Prospectus—A statement of a company's intent when it is planning to issue stocks for public sale. It includes disclosures which assist an investor in determining if the stock is a good investment.

Proxy—A form that when signed by an investor gives his voting power on his shares of stock to someone acting in his behalf.

Rally—If a stock is on the decline, it may experience a sudden rise due to some unforeseen happening. This is called a rally.

Spread—The difference between an asking price and a bidding price or a purchase and sell price.

Transfer Tax—A tax levied by some states that require tax to be paid on all transfers of stock from one person to another. The tax is usually nominal.

Turnover—The amount of volume on a particular day in either a specific stock or the market as a whole.

Yield—The return you can expect in the form of dividends on your investment in a specific company. To calculate yield, divide the total dividends paid the last year by the current market value. For those investing in stocks for the dividends rather than the long-range price increase of the stocks, the yield is very important.

Where to Begin

You have probably learned just enough in this chapter to get yourself into serious trouble if you attempt to invest in the stock market without further knowledge. That is why a broker is your best friend when you begin to break into the market.

But before you get a broker, learn more. A good way to start is to become a "paper stockholder." That is, you make a trial portfolio and follow it on paper only for a certain period of time. In this way, you can learn more about the stock market while experiencing the gains and losses (without really investing money) you can expect. Begin your paper portfolio by choosing stocks that you are familiar with. Perhaps you use some of the firm's products or you may know that a particular stock is continually a good investment. Do not discount the small company which may in the long run be the best growth stock. Include a wide range of different stocks. Diversify . . . an important word for all investors. It means simply, do not put all your money on one company. If the company stock declined, you could lose substantially. Hedge your investment with the purchase of a variety of stocks. Most brokers recommend that you do not invest more than 20 percent of your portfolio in any one stock, at least initially.

Decide on your paper investment. Say, $5000. With that $5000 buy (on paper) stocks like utilities, cosmetics, industries, banks, whatever you feel would be a good investment. "Feel" here is perhaps a bad word. You should never buy a stock on a hunch. You should base your decision on sound knowledge of the company and the directions it is going in and what it has planned for the future. There are several ways you can investigate a company. Many publications (some listed at the end of this chapter) provide news of companies, and all companies selling shares of stock to the public are required to issue financial statements at least once a year. These are available on request.

Once you have decided on the stock you wish to put into your paper portfolio, make a bargain with yourself. Either plan to sell on a given date or plan to sell when your stock reaches a certain price. In this way, you will be able to calculate the profits or losses you may have experienced in, say, six months. This paper exercise will give you added knowledge about companies and their actions in the market. Some companies you will undoubtedly wish to remove from your portfolio before you actually invest your money.

Resources

There are many places you can go to learn more about the stock market, notably a broker. However, before you take that step, acquaint yourself further with the market utilizing some or all of the following methods:

New York Stock Exchange. The Exchange will supply you on request with a pamphlet outlining in brief the background and function of the Exchange. Write to: The New York Stock Exchange, Investors Service Bureau, 11 Wall St., New York, NY 10005. No charge. A bibliography of books, newspapers and periodicals, reference works and services will usually be included.

An Investors Information Kit, $2. Write to: Publications Department, New York Stock Exchange, Inc., 11 Wall St., New York, NY 10005.

The Wall Street Journal. The financial newspaper. It lists daily the stocks traded on the New York Stock Exchange, the American Stock Exchange and over-the-counter stocks. Printed Monday through Friday, it can be purchased at newsstands or subscribed to at $28 a year. The *Journal* also prints company news, economic news and other news of importance to the financial community.

Barron's. Published weekly at a cost of $18 a year to the subscriber. Its format is basically the same as *The Wall Street Journal*. It is available on some newstands.

The Exchange Magazine. Published monthly by the New York Stock Exchange, it contains information on investing and the economy. The cost is $2.50 a year.

Standard and Poor's Stock Guide. This is published monthly and rates some 5000 companies on a basis of A to Z. Also offers statistics about these companies.

Investment Seminars. These are not uncommon anywhere in the United States. They are generally arranged by a brokerage house or bank. Watch your local paper or call several of the larger brokerage firms in your area.

College Classes. Most local colleges and even some night classes held at high schools offer investment courses designed to acquaint the beginner with the market. Check your local college or High School Extension Board.

Exchanges. If you are lucky enough to live close to one of the thirteen exchanges in the United States, then you have a wealth of information at your fingertips. All exchanges offer not only printed material on the operation of the exchange but guided tours of the exchange in operation. Don't miss this opportunity to see the market in action if you live near one of these.

A Woman's Money, How to Protect and Increase It in the Stock Market, by Catharine Brandt, is an excellent introduction for the beginning investor and written specifically with the woman in mind. Cornerstone Library, New York, 1970.

Libraries. There are thousands of books that offer information on the stock market. You have only to check the local library to discover that the information is seemingly endless.

7

Investing–Mutual Funds & Bonds

While investing in stocks is generally held to be the most popular way to increase your money dramatically—or diminish it just as dramatically—there are other methods of investing which, while earning you substantially more than a bank savings account, do so without the high risk found in investing in stocks. As is the way with investments, the lower the risk, the lower the return but the more sure the return. Some of the ways you can invest with a greater degree of safety include mutual funds and bonds.

Mutual Funds

Most closely related to the stock market game outlined in the previous chapter is the mutual fund. When you invest in mutual funds, you trust your money to a professional investment counselor who in turn buys stocks. Mutual funds are considered somewhat safer than plunging into the stock market on your own for a variety of reasons, but mainly because your money is not invested in any one stock *and* a professional investment counselor is "protector" of your savings. Many mutual funds have up to 100 stocks listed in their prospectus. Since your money is diversified in this manner (much more so than you could accomplish with just your money alone), there is less likelihood that you will lose your entire investment. Ideally, if one stock falls far short, another will compensate with a rise in price or at least a stability that will either minimize or eliminate your loss.

Mutual funds are good or bad, depending on who you ask. While one was noted to have increased 197 percent over an eleven-year period, 1964–1975, still another in that same period of time increased only 8 percent. Some feel mutual funds are safe. They are to the extent that you enjoy greater diversification for your money. However, mutual funds are no guarantee of profits as some would have you believe. You can protect your initial investment in some funds with built-in insurance but not all funds offer this.

There are some 600 mutual funds in existence today. Twenty-eight years ago, they were investing a meager $500,000 in the market. Today that has grown to almost $10 billion. These figures alone atest to the growing confidence in mutual funds.

Mutual funds were designed essentially for the long-range investor. You cannot expect a quick return on your money. As a matter of fact, most investors begin with a modest sum and add monthly to that until they have reached a goal—$10,000 is a popular investment total. Usually a new fund member is asked to contract for a certain investment, say $10,000, to be paid over a period of time. The investor cannot usually expect any return on her money until the contract is completed and the money has had time to work. Ten years is a good average.

Load and No Load Mutual Funds   There are basically two kinds of mutual funds—load and no load. The difference is the commission or *load*; the load fund charges commissions for their salesmen. The no-load fund does not usually involve a salesman and thus no commission is paid. Since sales commissions can be a big cut out of your investment (the investor, of course, pays), the no-load funds are most desirable. However, as things usually go, they are also harder to find. Of the 600 funds in the U.S., only 150 are no-load; finding those 150, especially one with shares available, can be difficult. Since no salesman is involved, no-load funds are basically found by "word of mouth." Your banker, stockbroker or a friend may know of one with shares for sale. Or you may run across an ad in *The Wall Street Journal*, *Forbes* magazine or your local newspaper.

If you think looking for a no-load fund may be too difficult, consider the alternative. With the load fund, the salesman gets his money *first*—some 9 percent of your investment. If your contract is for $10,000, that's $900, a sizable chunk. The commission alone is one of the reasons for the slow return on a mutual fund. It takes you several years to make up the difference and begin realizing any kind of profit.

Both load and no-load mutual funds are subject to an annual service fee and, of course, should the fund sell stock and reinvest, then there is a sales fee as well that must be distributed among the fundholders. This, again, takes a sizable chunk out of your investment.

Even with all these charges, the Mutual Fund has shown itself to be a "good" investment if you can wait for the rewards. With proper management, your initial investment should double within ten years. If you are fortunate enough to be in a no-load fund, perhaps even sooner than that.

Kinds of Mutual Funds

Once you decide to invest in a mutual fund, you will be offered a variety of plans within the fund. Choose the one best suited to your needs. The most common plans offered are: (1) the income fund, (2) the growth fund, (3) the speculative fund, and (4) the balanced fund.

The Income Fund consists of stocks that pay high dividends but do not necessarily show a marked increase or decrease in share value. In other words, you are investing your money more for the dividends you will receive annually than for the "killing" you might make if the stocks rose dramatically. These stocks are generally "safe." Being "safe," you cannot expect to make any dramatic increases in your investment.

Growth Funds invest in growth stocks. These stocks are considered "high risk" but potentially "high income." They usually pay no dividends but if their growth potential is realized, your initial investment could increase dramatically over a short period of time.

A Speculative Fund consists of very high risk stocks. You could lose all or double or triple your money in a relatively short period of time. Compared to speculative funds, the growth fund is "safe."

Balanced Funds are thought to be the safest of all mutual fund plans. The portfolio consists of a balance of bonds, preferred stocks, and common stocks as a protection against any sharp decline in any one area. Dividends are usually healthy and the investor can expect a modest but regular return on her money. This fund is designed for those who wish to have a regular income after the fund has had time to grow.

Mutual Funds as an Investment

There are a variety of methods of investing in mutual funds, most of which cater to the small investor (the investor who cannot afford to lay down $10,000 but can afford to make monthly payments toward that investment). Some methods open to you include: (1) automatic deduction afforded by most banks, (2) payroll deduction offered by some companies, (3) reinvestment of all dividends you receive from a mutual fund of which you are already a member, and (4) contracting on a down payment and agreed-on monthly payments until the total is reached.

Although the mutual fund is not completely secure it is considered a good investment for the new investor, one who does not know the stock market well. This new investor is assured that her funds will be invested intelligently and will, therefore, be more likely to reap some rewards. Some have compared it to the investment club as money is pooled to make your investment worth more on the market. That, however, is where the comparison ceases. The mutual fund affords you no choice about where your money will be invested except for the very broad general plans offered.

Some real advantages that you can expect from investing in mutual funds include:

Diversification—Your money will be invested in many different stocks, more than you would most likely be able to invest in on your own. In this way, the likelihood of loss is less, for if one stock falls it is conceivable that another will rise or at least hold firm.

Professional Management—You do not have to spend hours instructing yourself about the stock market. You are hiring someone to do the thinking for you, someone who has had a great deal of experience in dealing with stocks.

Liquidity—With most mutual funds, you can sell at any time simply by expressing a desire to do so.

Monthly Payment Plan—For the new investor or the investor with limited capital, the mutual fund affords the opportunity to invest monthly a sum in keeping with income.

Federally Regulated—According to Federal law, mutual funds must pass on to the investor a minimum of 90 percent of income.

Resources—How to Find a Mutual Fund

Performance should be your main criterion for selecting a fund as you are in this to make money. How has the fund fared over the past ten years? If it has been in existence for less than that time, then be more skeptical. Make certain that it has some redeeming factor to make up for its lack of experience. Ideally, you will find a fund through a friend who is already a satisfied member; through your broker who, even though he does not get the sales commission and will most probably lose some business because of it, should be willing to direct you to a "good" fund; or through your attorney or banker whose judgment you trust. If you do not find one in these ways, there are other avenues open to you. Check the following:

The Local Newspaper Most local newspapers list the ask and bid price of mutual funds traded that day. This will give you some idea of how many shares you can afford. Also you can assume that those demanding higher prices for their shares have a performance background equal to the increase over the other funds. While not a good reason by itself to buy the fund, you can use this as a basis for further investigation into funds.

Annual Report and Prospectus All mutual funds will be happy to comply with your request for an annual report and prospectus. These will give you a clue to the fund's performance. Also these reports list the stocks in which your money would be invested. Check them against what you know to be safe or high risk in the market.

Forbes Magazine This magazine publishes an issue on funds once a year—August. Highly informative.

Barron's This is a weekly financial paper available at newsstands and by subscription. Once and sometimes twice a month, *Barron's* publishes a performance average of more than 300 of the leading funds. Included are the yearly as well as the weekly percentage gains and losses.

Investment Companies, a book available at your library. Published by Arthur Wiesenberger Service Division of John Nuveen and Company, it lists most all funds, their past and present performance.

Fundscope, published monthly and dealing with fund news. Write to Fundscope, Suite 700, 1900 Avenue of the Stars, Los Angeles, CA 90067.

Johnson Investment Company Charts, a book available at your library. Performance charts on all the major funds. It affords easy comparison between funds through use of charts.

Mutual Fund Forum, published bi-monthly by The Investment Company Institute, 1775 K Street, N. W., Washington, DC 20006. This is the trade publication of most of the funds. It publishes statistics and general information on the industry.

Bonds

A high quality bond is the safest way to invest your money next to bank savings accounts and time certificates. Essentially, when you buy a bond, you lend money. In return, the borrower promises to pay you the face value of the bond plus a certain amount of interest. You might call a bond an I.O.U. to you, the lender. There are many different kinds of bonds; some extremely safe; others, not so safe.

Over 2000 bonds are listed on the New York Stock Exchange. Included among these are corporate bonds issued by companies that may or may not have stocks listed on the Exchange, U.S. Government bonds, bonds issued by foreign countries and New York City municipal bonds. Depending on the type of bond, denominations can range from $25 to $10,000 or more. The norm is $1000.

Types of Bonds Bonds come in two different types—bearer and serial. A *bearer* bond belongs to the person who has actual possession of it. The name of the purchaser is not on the bond at all. This type of bond can be considered the same as cash. If lost or stolen, there is no way to replace them and no way to identify them. A *serial* bond is just the opposite. It bears the purchaser's name and can be replaced if lost or stolen. Each serial bond has its own number, identifying it.

Interest rates on bonds vary, according to their reliability. There are some highly speculative bonds (bonds issued by companies that are not yet stable) that offer interest rates as high as 10 percent while the highly safe U.S. Savings Bonds offer only 6 percent, at maturity. In some cases where interest rates are low, it might be more beneficial to invest the money in a bank time certificate—but first you must consider the tax breaks available to you on some of these low-interest bonds, such as government and municipal bonds. The moral is: check a bond out thoroughly before buying. Just because it is a *bond* and not a stock does not mean it is safe. And a low interest rate does not mean it is a bad investment. Look into all the benefits before jumping into or out of a bond buy.

Rating Bonds Aside from the recommendation of your stockbroker, you can get more information on the risk value of a specific bond, either municipal or corporate, from two good sources: Moody's and Standard & Poor's. These ratings are available through your stockbroker. Both rate bonds from triple A to C, with triple A being the highest rating. It is recommended that the new investor put her money only in those rated A or above. Check both sources before you invest your money as ratings may vary.

Kinds of Bonds Available

Basically, there are three different types of bonds—U.S. Savings Bonds, municipal bonds and corporate bonds. There are offshoots of these such as bond funds, U.S. Treasury Bills and U.S. Treasury Bonds, but for the sake of discussion here, we will cover only the first three mentioned. Most of these offshoots require an initial investment, some as high as $10,000, to which few women just beginning to exercise their financial independence have access.

U.S. Savings Bonds By far the least expensive and most popular of all bonds issued in the United States, the U.S. Savings Bond owes much of its popularity to its denominations and the fine savings plans instituted around it. U.S. Savings Bonds are offered in two series, Series E and Series H. Most Americans are familiar with Series E. Series E bonds are issued in denominations as low as $25 and as high as $10,000. These bonds earn 6 percent and the purchase price is discounted to reflect the interest. In other words, a $25 bond sells for $18.75; in five years, the bond matures to a value of $25.20. A $50 bond sells for $37.50; a $75 for $56.25; a $100 for $75; a $200 for $150; a $500 for $375.00; a $1,000 for $750.00 and a $10,000 for $7,500.

One of the advantages offered the U.S. Savings Bond purchaser is cashing privileges. Series E bonds can be cashed in two months after their purchase. Of course, if you cash early, the interest rate is not as great and in some cases, there will be no interest at all. But at least you know if you need the money in a hurry, there is no hassle in getting it. Cashing a Series E bond is as simple as walking into the nearest bank. Buying one is just as simple. This is one of the greatest advantages of this particular bond. It is not only easily accessible to all the American public in terms of price but purchasing one is accomplished with ease. Many employers have instituted automatic savings plans where with just a signature on a form, a portion of your paycheck will be used to buy savings bonds each month. This kind of "forced" savings is essential for many Americans who if given half the chance will spend every penny they earn. The philosophy behind this type of savings plan is "if you never see the money, you will not miss it." For some, it works.

One of the advantages of putting your money in a savings bond, either Series E or Series H, is that the interest is exempt from all state and local income or personal property tax. They are not exempt, however, from federal income tax. Any interest must be reported in the year it is received. In the case of the Series E, this is when the bond is cashed. For the Series H, however, it is annual.

Series H bonds are bought at face value and interest paid annually by check. For example, if you buy a $500 Series H bond, you pay $500 for the bond and you receive an interest check each year from the government. Series H bonds mature in ten years. Denominations are $500, $1000, $5000 and $10,000. The interest rate is 6 percent, the same as the Series E bonds. Series H bonds are not as easy to obtain as Series E. You cannot buy them from the local bank. They can be bought at any Federal Reserve Bank or branch. They may be cashed there as well. Cashing privileges for the Series H bonds are the same as the Series E with the exception that there is a waiting period of six months from the date of purchase before they can be cashed.

Both Series E and Series H bonds are serial bonds. If lost or stolen, they will be replaced immediately by the government. Also there is no possibility of default. Both series are backed by the government. Your money is safe as long as the government functions and, after all, if it ceased to function, *every* investment would go down with it.

One of the disadvantages of U.S. Savings Bonds is that they do not increase with the rate of inflation. In other words, if you invested $500 in 1975, when the bond reached maturity in 1980 the rate of inflation may have decreased the value of that $500 so much that even the interest would not make up the difference. Savings bonds are not known for their high yield but rather for their safety and tax exempt status.

Municipal Bonds   There are over 50,000 municipal bonds on the market. When you invest in a municipal bond, you invest in a community or state. Municipal bonds are issued by cities to build schools, housing,or any number of other services needed within a city. The same type of purpose may apply to a state issue of municipal bonds. The single most attractive value of the municipal bond is its tax exempt status. Unlike the U.S. Savings Bond, it is exempt from all taxes, state, local and federal. The municipal bond, however, even though it is city or state backed is not entirely free from default. Look at the problems of New York City or any number of other U.S. cities that have experienced difficulties with budgets in the past years.

Municipal bonds may carry a maturity date from five to forty years. Interest usually ranges around 7 percent with higher interest rates offered on the more speculative issues. Denominations are $1000 and upwards, with the $5000 denomination being the most popular. Municipal bonds are sold at face value with interest paid at a specified time, every month, six months or year. Most municipal bonds are bearer bonds. At the designated time that the interest is due, you clip a coupon from the bond and cash it in to get your interest. Usually this can be handled through your bank. Once again, though, the bearer bond is highly dangerous. It should be treated as you would cash. Lose it and you have lost your investment.

Corporate Bonds These bonds pay the highest rate of interest, some going as high as 10 percent. It follows that they are the highest risk. By buying a corporate bond, you are lending money to a company. Should that company fail, you lose your money. Your investment, however, is safer in bonds than it would be if you bought stock in the company. The law says that if a company should fail, its bondholders are paid first, then preferred stockholders and finally, common stockholders.

As a bondholder in a corporation, you have no say in the company as you would if you owned common stock. You are simply a creditor of the company, nothing more.

Corporate bonds can mature in six months or thirty years from the date of purchase. They can be (1) straight bonds—meaning you receive interest as agreed with no stipulations put on either the interest or the bond; (2) they can be recallable—meaning that the corporation reserves the right to call in the bonds after a certain period of time. For example, if you bought a bond that matures in twenty years but the company reserved the right to recall after five years, you would be required to sell the bond back to the company in five years if they should exercise the recall. Generally, if a company does recall a bond, it pays the face value of the bond plus a year's interest, giving the bondholder a nice profit; (3) bonds can be convertible—meaning that after a certain period of time, the bondholder can trade the bond in on a certain number of shares of stock in the company. This is an added option that makes corporate bonds attractive, especially if you are interested in a particular company but want to watch it for a while before putting your money in stocks.

Some corporate bonds are traded on the stock market. It is rare that a corporate bond stays in the hands of the initial purchaser until maturity. Corporate bonds promise a high rate of return on your money with high interest rates paid annually. For further information, ask your stockbroker.

Jargon You Should Know

The following are some terms relating to bonds and mutuals you might find helpful.

Accrued Interest—Accumulated Interest. If you buy a bond, you must pay the interest to the seller from the time of the last interest payment to the present. You will be reimbursed at the end of the interest quarter when you receive the interest for the entire quarter or year, whichever applies. The same holds true if you are the seller.

Amortize. A bond that provides for the repayment of the loan over a certain period of time designated at the time of purchase. A $10,000 bond, for example, may be paid off in increments of $2500 over a period of ten years.

Bearer Bond. A bond is assumed to be the property of the person who has it in their possession.

Callable Bond. Bonds that include a provision enabling the issuer to recall the bond after a certain period of time. For example, a company may issue a twenty-year bond, callable after five years.

Convertible Bond. A bond that can be converted into stock in the company. Usually limitations concerning when this may be done and how much stock can be purchased are noted in the bond.

Coupon. As its name implies, a coupon attached to a bond. Coupons are clipped to redeem interest on the bond. These coupons are typical on the bearer municipal bond. Coupons may designate a dollar amount and can be cashed at your local bank or brokerage house.

Current Yield. To calculate the current yield of a bond, divide the selling price into the interest. Thus a bond selling for $1000 with an interest annually of $80 would have a current yield of 8 percent. The same bond selling at $800 would have a current yield of 10 percent. At $1200, a current yield of 6.7 percent. The yield then moves in the opposite direction of the bond price. If the price goes up, the yield goes down and vice versa. Depending on your needs, a high yield may or may not be a factor in purchasing a particular bond.

Debenture Bond. An issue that is backed only be general credit of the corporation. No collateral is offered.

Denomination. Face amount of a savings bond, e.g., the lowest denomination of a Series E bond is $25.00.

Discount Bond. A bond selling for less than the face value.

First Mortgage Bond. A corporate bond that is secured by a mortgage on a portion or all of the property of the corporation.

Issue Price. The price at which the bond is offered for sale.

Maturity. Date on which the bond becomes due and payable.

Premium Bond. A bond selling above the face value.

Principal. Face value of a bond.

Revenue Bond. A municipal bond dependent on the revenue received from a public facility to repay the loan, i.e., a bridge, a road or mass transit.

Serial Bonds. Bonds which bear a name of the purchaser. These types of bonds can be replaced if lost or stolen.

Spread. The difference between the asked and bid price, specifically on a bond.

Tax Exempt. Bonds which enjoy tax-free status, some from only state and local tax; others from those as well as federal tax.

Term. The period of time for which a bond is issued, e.g., a five-year bond; a twenty-five-year bond.

Resources

U.S. Government Printing Office, Public Documents Dept., Washington, DC 20402—pamphlets on U.S. Savings Bonds.

Local Bank—information on U.S. Savings Bonds.

Local Federal Reserve Bank—information on Series H savings bonds. Federal Reserve Banks are located in the following cities:

Boston, MA 02106; New York, NY 10045; Buffalo, NY 14240; Philadelphia, PA 19101; Cleveland, OH 44101; Cincinnati, OH 45201; Pittsburgh, PA 15230; Richmond, VA 23213; Baltimore, MD 21203; Charlotte, NC 28201; Atlanta, GA 30303; Birmingham, AL 35202; Jacksonville, FL 32203; Nashville, TN 37203; New Orleans, LA 70160; Chicago, IL 60690; Detroit, MI 48231; St. Louis, MO 63166; Little Rock, AR 72203; Louisville, KY 40201; Memphis, TN 38101; Minneapolis, MN 55480; Helena, MT 59601; Kansas City, KA 64198; Denver, CO 80217; Oklahoma City, OK 73125; Omaha, NB 68102; Dallas, TX 75222; El Paso, TX 79999; Houston, TX 77001; San Antonio, TX 78295; San Francisco, CA 94120; Los Angeles, CA 90051; Portland, OR 97208; Salt Lake City, UT 84110; Seattle, WA 98124.

Local government office—city municipal bonds available.

Stockbroker—corporate bond information.

8

Writing a Will

If you die today, who will get the proceeds from your insurance policy? Who will inherit that diamond necklace, the one good piece of jewelry you have? If you have children, who will care for them? Who would *you* like to have care for them? Over half of all Americans who own property die without a will. Who then inherits? Usually the next of kin. Oftentimes, it can be the one person you do not want to receive what you have worked so hard to make.

No one really thinks they will die. Writing a will is something you can do "someday, when the time is right" but not today. Think how often you have heard on the late news about a woman in her twenties who was killed in an auto accident or an airplane crash, or died from a heart attack or cancer. It does happen, and as healthy as you might feel right now, it could happen to you; to me. We must recognize the fact of death. Think of the alternatives—Aunt Mattie inheriting the family jewels (you just know she will sell them at the first opportunity)—or, heaven forbid, your ex-husband collecting your life insurance or inheriting what little wealth you have managed to accumulate on your own.

So, you are convinced; you need to make a will. The next problem is what to put in it. Most women feel that they do not own enough to bother with a will and in the majority of cases, as women are only beginning to insist on their monetary as well as their human rights, the truth is that most of them do have little to put in a will. But whatever your status, you do have something—probably more than you realize.

Take an accounting of your belongings, both personal holdings and those which you might hold with someone else. Do you have jewelry that is valuable, either sentimental value or real value? Do you have a secret cache of money? Do you own property, jointly or alone? Do you have a life insurance policy?

Who would you like to care for any dependent children? Do you wish to make certain that a close relative does not inherit anything? Do you own antiques, rare books or coins that others might not recognize as being valuable?

There are many factors to consider when you actually sit down to make a will. The first thing you have to do is decide for yourself exactly what is important to you. Wills are meant to not only ease the burden of grieving relatives but, most important, to make certain that what happens to your personal possessions is what *you* want. A will is the only way to be sure that is made clear.

What Kind of Will?

The best of all possible wills is one drawn up by an attorney. Then you are certain that the state laws are taken into account and that it is a legal document that, barring any unforeseen happening, will be followed to the letter after your death. An attorney is no guarantee but it is as close as you can get to certainty. Attorney fees are minimal, from $50 to $250, considering the peace of mind you will have, especially if it is imperative in your mind that your personal belongings be distributed properly. Many people save themselves a dollar by drawing up a will themselves. This is not necessarily bad. If the document is handwritten, with no strikeovers or erasures, and is properly witnessed, it can be as binding as the attorney-drawn will. However, note that more handwritten wills have been contested and "thrown out" than the attorney variety.

State laws regarding inheritance vary and without the expert assistance of an attorney you may will something that you cannot legally will. You may not comply with the minimum bequest to a next-of-kin as designated by the law or you may leave a bequest in such a way that the taxes will virtually leave the inheritor with nothing. The safest way is to let the attorney do it. She knows how to leave the most to the inheritor and the least to the tax collector.

What to Put in Your Will

The first thing you must do in a will is *identify* yourself: "I, Mavis E. Arthur Groza of 1567 Stanford St., Santa Rosa, California . . ." This first paragraph should also include a statement of your *intent to make a will* and a *statement revoking any previous wills* you might have made. Next you must *provide for your funeral*. Burial expenses have first claim against the estate, as do your current debts, taxes and costs of administering the will. It is a courtesy to your relatives if you designate how and where you wish to be buried. As a matter of fact, it is even more of a help if you arrange your own funeral. This is not an uncommon practice these days. It requires only a telephone call to the funeral home of your choice to arrange an appointment to discuss how you would like your funeral arranged, then note this in your will. Unless you designate otherwise in your will, the costs of your burial, current debts, taxes and administration costs will be charged equally to all the beneficiaries.

Next comes the "guts" of your will, your chance to make your wishes known after you are dead as to the *dispersal of your possessions*.

In your will, you should also *name an executor*, someone who will administer the will and see that your wishes are carried out. This may be your lawyer, a bank, your wife, a friend, whoever you think will be willing to accept the task and who will, most importantly, see that the will is adhered to completely. Costs of administering the will can be substantial. To avoid these costs as much as possible, husbands often name wives and wives, husbands as executor. Close relatives could also be named to save on costs, provided they are willing to accept the responsibility. If the estate is fairly large, however, it is a good idea to name an expert who will have the time and knowledge to administer the will to save on taxes and other costs.

Your will may also include a provision for a trust, a sum of money set aside and allotted over an extended period of time to an inheritor who is either too young to handle the money or who is financially inexperienced and thus likely to mishandle a large sum. Your will should also provide for any minor children, their education, etc.

Disposing of Your Possessions When it comes time to decide exactly what to put into the will in the way of personal belongings, use the following as a guide.

Do you have jewelry that is valuable? Most women have some piece of jewelry that means something special to them, whether it is valuable or not. A gift from a friend, your wedding ring, your mother's ring or maybe it's just a pin you picked up on a trip that has come to mean something far beyond its value. What do you want to happen to these valuables when you die? Do you want them just thrown in with the rest of your personal belongings, to be given to the next-of-kin or disposed of by relatives who just do not care as much about these things as you do? Who would appreciate them as you have?

Do you have a secret cache of money? It could be a savings account or checking account or some bonds or stocks stashed away in a safe deposit box. If you do and you do not leave a will, your heirs may never find them. Every year banks open safe deposit boxes and discover thousands of dollars in bonds, stocks and even cash. If the rightful owner or heirs cannot be found, the contents are disposed of in a manner prescribed by law. This usually means that the state gets it. Is that what you want to happen to what you worked so hard to save? It is up to you. Savings accounts and checking accounts go the same way if not claimed. Bank charges (even on savings accounts after a certain period of time) will eat up your cash slowly but surely and you will not be around to do anything about it.

Do you own property? If you own property in your name only, then it is your sole responsibility and right to designate who will inherit. You will save your heirs many problems if you let your desires be known. If the property is of any value at all, and what property is not these days, it will more than anything else bring out those relatives who do not particularly care about you but who can smell cash when your coffin is shut. Do you want the property sold and the money divided between loved ones? If you want it to stay in the family, who can best comply with these wishes? Who would feel the way you do about keeping the land even though the income from selling it may be tempting?

Who would you like to care for any dependent children you leave behind? Generally, the wishes of the woman are honored over a husband's if both should die at the same time. If you do not make your wishes known, relatives may cause the children unnecessary pain by battling over them. It is the one positive thing you can do for your children and it may mean the difference between what you consider a proper atmosphere and one that is detrimental to the emotional and physical health of your children.

Do you have antiques, rare books, paintings or coins? There is always the possibility that some relative with an untrained eye for value may get among your things and throw out valuable possessions if you do not indicate their value in your will. While the possibility may seem laughable to you who are well aware of the value, it does happen and it could happen to your things.

Do you have an insurance policy? In most cases, if you are working, you have a life insurance policy and you probably designated who you wanted to be beneficiary in your first days on the job. Have you checked that policy lately? Is the beneficiary you named initially the one you still wish to name? If not, change it. Did you bother to name one at all? Sometimes, the company you work for will assume that you wish your next-of-kin to receive the proceeds. If you are married, that means your husband.

How will the money from the policy be paid? Many people assume that it must be paid in a lump sum. This is not true. You can direct the insurance company to pay only a portion at the time of death and the remainder at a time in the future. Or you can direct them to pay the interest only with the principal amount held until some future time designated by you. It is your insurance and you can do what you want with it.

Do you know how much life insurance you have? Many women do not. Work policies are often accepted without bothering to find out just how much is involved. Find out. For most women, this insurance policy is probably the biggest part of their estate; something that important should have a dollar figure on it.

If your insurance policy designates a beneficiary, then you do not include it in your will. You have already let your wishes be known. However, you can designate that the insurance money be paid to the estate, not to any person. Then you can divide the money any way you like among your loved ones. The one drawback in doing this is that as a part of your estate, it will become just that much more expensive disposing of the additional assets, not to mention the taxes that will be levied against it.

Insurance, whether you designate a beneficiary or have it included in the estate, is, for tax purposes, included in the total value of your estate. However, there is a way to avoid paying taxes on your insurance monies. The law states that insurance monies must be taxed "if the policy was owned and paid for by the person whose life was insured'' or if he had direct control of the policy and its eventual distribution. If someone else buys and controls the policy, it cannot be taxed as part of your estate. Thus, if your husband, daughter, mother or whoever, takes out a policy on your life, the proceeds are theirs on your death, free from any estate tax. This seems the only sensible way to arrange an insurance policy. After all, it is your loved one you want to provide for when you die, not the tax collector.

If you are married, do you own property jointly with your husband? Not all states have the same laws governing property owned by both husband and wife. In some states, even though your name may be on the deed, the property in essence belongs to your husband. If he dies first, which the odds say he will, he determines who will inherit. In most cases, the wife is entitled to and gets half, the remainder usually going to children. This is not true in all states. In nine states (Arizona, California, Hawaii, Idaho, Louisiana, Nevada, New Mexico, Texas and Washington) there are community property laws. This means that all property bought after the marriage belongs to both the husband and wife equally and the wife can thus designate her half after her death. Even though this might sound equitable enough, note that the husband can dispose of or transfer the property while he and his wife are still alive and he can do so without the consent of the wife. He is, as a general rule, considered the manager of the property, advising his wife only after he has completed the transaction. Assuming, however, that your husband will not do this, if you live in any one of the nine states, you can include your half of the property in your will.

If you live in one of the other forty-one states, you are generally just as much a non-person when it comes to wills as you are when it comes to credit. You can write a will but if your husband outlives you, it is virtually invalid, except for your personal belongings. You cannot will property or cash or stocks or bonds since they are more than likely in both your names or in his alone. If they are in your name alone, it's a different story. Then they are yours to do with as you wish. But in the majority of cases, the only thing you have that truly belongs to you if you are married are your personal belongings—your jewelry, fur coat or banking accounts in your name only.

In the case of wills as in the case of most other things in the world, men rule. Marriage means that the husband is the provider, the wife only one who benefits. Thus, all things belong to the husband. Such laws that allow this have been predicated on the belief that women do not know how to handle money, that they will squander it or that they will allow some fast-talking man to take it from them and they will be left with nothing. Such may have been the case a hundred years ago when women were mere chattels, and most content to be so, but not today. Some of the laws have not caught up with the time, however, and women still do not realize their equal rights to an estate. If this is so in your state, make the most of what you have.

Gifts Before You Die

If you are fortunate enough to enjoy many assets—money as well as property, stocks and bonds—then perhaps the wisest thing for you to do is to begin to dispose of them while you still live. Gift taxes are about 25 percent lower than estate tax rates. (Some estate taxes can be as much as two thirds or three fourths of the larger estates.) A well-planned system of gifts can allow you to distribute your money tax free. In fact, you might save money on your own income tax doing this.

During your lifetime, according to present gift tax laws (1976), you can give a total of $30,000 during your lifetime to any one or a number of people, free of federal gift tax. In addition, you can distribute an additional sum of $3000 each year to such people as you decide. The lifetime allowance of $30,000 can be given within a year or over a period of years and the $3000 a year per beneficiary can continue yearly for as long as you live. If you are married, the amounts double to $6000 a year and $60,000 over a lifetime for both yourself and your husband. If you give more than the allowable amounts, you must file a gift tax return and pay the necessary taxes due. If you left the same amounts in your will to the designated people, state and federal estate taxes would have to be paid, thus lowering considerably the amount of the bequest. Besides, why wait? If you have the money and are not in need of it to support yourself, why not enjoy sharing it with someone you care about while you are still alive.

There is one catch to this method of disposing of your estate. If a gift is made within three years of your death, the federal Treasury Department can decide that the gift was "in contemplation of death." If this can be proven, then the gift is subject to the higher estate tax. Heirs can always fight this move by the Tax Department and there is always a good likelihood that they will win. It is, however, a possible action you should be aware of and should make your heirs aware of, just in case.

Leaving Money in Trust   If a minor child or another loved one is involved who you feel is not capable of handling a large sum of money for one reason or another, then you have the option of leaving the money in a trust account for them. Simply, this involves setting a certain amount of money aside with instructions to pay the beneficiary in a certain way. Methods of payment vary but may include: (1) payment of interest only during the person's lifetime with the principal to go to someone else on the beneficiary's death, (2) payment of interest until the beneficiary reaches a certain age at which time the beneficiary receives all of the money in the trust, (3) payment of interest and a portion of the principal until all the trust is dissipated, (4) any other method you desire.

While a good method for holding money for someone, this method involves hiring someone to handle the trust for you, usually a bank or trust company. This, of course, involves using a certain amount of the trust fund for fees. These fees, however, are usually minor compared to the peace of mind you will experience in knowing that you have provided for a loved one until they are capable of doing so for themselves.

Can You Disinherit Someone?   You should enlist the assistance of a lawyer to disinherit members of your family. In most cases, you cannot disinherit a surviving husband, even if you are not living together, unless you do it with strict adherence to the laws in your particular state. You lawyer can advise you on this. In some states, a husband is entitled to one third or more of his wife's estate. In some cases, this cannot be overcome. However, even if you must leave a portion to your husband, you can leave it in such a way that he will not benefit much from the income . . . in the form of a trust that pays interest only for his lifetime. How you disinherit a member of your family must be legally correct or they can contest the will and win. The services of a lawyer are imperative if you desire to disinherit; a lawyer can also help find ways to leave the least amount to the tax collector.

9

Financing Your Way Through a Divorce

Some believe that the happiest moment in a woman's life is her marriage day, a day second only to the birth of her first child. Perhaps it is the day cherished by most women . . . the day they surrendered themselves totally to the man they loved. And perhaps it is that great happiness which accounts for the total unhappiness felt when that love no longer exists. Divorce means an end to all the great and beautiful things you believed possible with this man. It can only mean pain to all those involved no matter how the relationship may have deteriorated.

Recognizing the reality of divorce is a small death that one never fully recovers from, but for those smart enough to build on the experience, it is something that you can learn from, something that hopefully will help you to understand yourself better and know your needs more completely.

Divorce is a lonely thing. Friends will say polite things which may make you feel even more alone, and you will find emotions you thought were either nonexistent or buried. If you are lucky, your soon-to-be ex-husband will be kind, understanding and concerned about your well-being and it will all end amicably with no shouting or hurting. If like many others you are not lucky, the divorce may turn into a nightmare of threats, shouts and even physical encounters. While the harder of the two, the latter way, in the long run, may be the best—at least you will be able to rationalize forgetting much sooner.

Once the relationship is ended, whether the legal formalities are a reality yet or not, many women rush headlong into another relationship. Forgetting to stop and assess how they really feel, they become aware only of their need to be wanted—by someone. Theirs is a frantic search for warmth in the world. Try not to fall prey to this disease of the divorced. Look on divorce as another beginning, a time to find *yourself*. Chances are the marriage now ending was something you rushed into, out of need, desire or blind love. Make the next relationship better by finding yourself first.

Divorce is never pleasant, but it can be bearable and you can survive it emotionally. Know first of all that you are not alone. Divorce has almost become the American way of life. It is not a good part of that life. Divorce has become an "easy out" for many people. Who has not heard someone say, "If it doesn't work out, we can always get a divorce." More and more couples are taking the "out" every year. In the 1890s only 6 percent of the marriages ended in divorce. In 1960 the rate was 22 percent; and in 1972 it had jumped to 40 percent. Today it is close to 50 percent and still climbing. That means that the odds are only fifty-fifty that your marriage will survive and if the trend continues, soon the odds will be against its survival.

The Lawyer's Role

Financially, divorce can be fatal. Many lawyers who make their living on divorce thrive on the dissension between husband and wife. It is this dissension and bitterness that will keep the litigations in the court longer and thus the lawyer's bill higher. Divorce costs can run anywhere from $200 to thousands of dollars, depending on your attorney and how much he thinks "the traffic will bear." That is not to say that all lawyers are out to make a killing on your divorce, only that the rates may vary sharply. Make certain that the financial arrangements are agreed on before you actually hire a lawyer.

More than likely, this will be your first encounter with an attorney. It must, therefore, be someone you can trust. She is, after all, working not only to free you but to free you with an equal share of what you and your husband have accumulated over the years. The best possible way to find an attorney is, of course, through your own personal contacts, either an attorney who is a friend or one recommended by a friend. If, however, you are not fortunate enough to learn of a reputable attorney this way, then rely on the local Bar Association. You can locate it in the telephone book yellow pages under Attorney Referral Service. The Bar Association referral service will not only suggest an attorney but arrange for you to talk to her or him for one half-hour for a nominal fee, before you hire.

If you prefer a woman attorney, you need only say so to the Bar Association. Women attorneys can also be found through local Women's Centers and chapters of feminists organizations, such as NOW (National Organization for Women). A woman attorney, especially one who has been through a divorce herself, should be supportive in most cases.

If money is a real problem, the Legal Aid Society does help some of those who are unable to pay. Look in your telephone book for the number of the local office.

One Attorney or Two

Ideally, both parties involved will agree almost totally on all things and one attorney can handle the divorce. It is possible and definitely much more sound a proposal on a financial level. Unfortunately, it seldom seems possible. You should not, however, discount the possibility without first discussing it with your husband. If you both can agree on the division of any property, cash, stocks, bonds, etc., and the care of the children, then one attorney is a natural way to do it. You simply both visit him, advise him of how you wish the divorce handled in terms of possessions and the rest is relatively simple. It's the haggling over possessions that causes the lawyer's bill to get higher and higher. Even in states where divorce is hampered by proving one party at fault, this type of arrangement is possible. If both parties can agree, then one brings the divorce action and the other simply does not contest.

No-Fault Divorce

A few states are liberalizing their divorce laws. Some are of the mind that this is one of the factors causing the increase in divorce. It has become "too easy." Actually for those involved in the divorce action, it is the only civilized way to approach a situation that had become unbearable. The new system is called no-fault divorce. California notably has established grounds of "irreconcilable differences" which have brought about an "irremediable breakdown of the marriage." Neither party must be proved wrong. In fact, no wrong must be proved; the marriage simply did not work. Other states still cling to antiquated grounds such as mental or physical cruelty, desertion, nonsupport, alcohol, felonies, impotency, pregnancy at marriage, drug addiction, fraudulent contract, incompatibility, fraud, force and insanity—not to mention adultery.

Alimony and Child Support While the growing trend toward no-fault divorce may make it easier both emotionally and physically to obtain a divorce, it also carries with it certain liberalized attitudes toward alimony and child custody. No longer does the wife automatically get alimony. No longer is it automatically assumed that the children may best be cared for by the mother. Courts are now making these decisions on an equal basis. If the woman, for example, is working and receiving a salary that has been supporting the family while the man has been home, disabled, going to school or whatever, it is possible that the woman will end up paying alimony to the man until he establishes himself. The likelihood of this happening is not great since men are traditionally the breadwinners in most families, but the possibility is definitely there.

As far as any children involved, the court may decide that the husband is better able to care for them than the mother. The reasons for this decision may vary from the woman's lack of interest in caring for them to her inability to care for them emotionally or financially. No longer can you assume that the children will be given to the woman.

What to Live On in the Meantime

You have made the decision to divorce. Now what do you do? Generally, a woman will have a job; most women do these days. However, it is unlikely that the job will be bringing in enough money to meet the household expenses and bills. Your very first action should be to have your attorney get a court order directing your husband to pay child support if there are children involved and alimony until you get on your feet. It is even possible to get an injunction preventing your husband from dissipating your assets.

Generally, the woman gets the house, especially if there are children involved. The husband may continue to make the payments until the divorce action is final. This should not be assumed, however; get your attorney to have it included in the court order.

If you decide to leave, then you have the problem of setting up housekeeping elsewhere and you will find youself confronted with apartment deposits, security deposits to the electric company, the telephone company and anyone else with whom you try to establish credit. That is, you will find yourself with these problems if you have not established your own credit during your marriage (see chapter on Credit). Whatever you decide to do, you can obtain a court order temporarily directing your husband to assist you, depending, of course, on what type of job, if any, you are holding down. Do not, however, expect large and extended payments from your ex-husband. Things are just not happening like that any more. Men would at one time have expected to pay half or more of their yearly salary to an ex-wife. This generally is no longer true. Women are expected to contribute something to their own support if they are physically able. If they have no training, then the court will in some cases direct the ex-husband to pay for any schooling required to train the woman for a particular job. More and more the equality that women have worked so hard to obtain is becoming a reality. In the case of divorce, some who have been accustomed to large alimony grants may find it to their detriment . . . that is, if they had any ideas of sitting back and enjoying their leisure at their husband's expense.

On the other side, more and more women are refusing to accept alimony payments. They do not need them. They can make it on their own. They need not be dependent any more. That, by far, is the best possible way. If, however, you need the alimony to make it initially, do not be too proud to ask for or accept it. It is your right and your husband's duty to see that you are in a position to fend for yourself before he leaves you totally.

Does Mrs. Brown Disappear?

When Mr. Brown leaves, does Mrs. Brown disappear? Legally, no, not until the divorce is final. However, to the credit world, she ceases to exist. She will most likely find herself confronted with letters requesting the return of any credit cards she holds in the name of *Mrs*. Brown. Not only that, she will probably have difficulty obtaining, from the same companies, credit in her own name. Even though it is she who has been paying the bills (this is generally the case in most households), it is the husband who has the credit, not her. She must re-establish herself, a task that may seem impossible. The creditors will require references—like a job that she has had for a year or more, a checking and/or savings account in her own name, and credit references in her own name. Most of these and usually all are hard for a newly divorced woman to come by. Only a few can qualify. Thus, you must be content with no credit for a while until you establish yourself or you will have to resort to asking a friend to co-sign for you, sometimes a humiliation to a woman who looks on herself as anything but a beginner in life. If you are smart, you will prepare for the eventuality of divorce by creating your credit before it happens.

In essence, you can say that *Mrs.* Brown does disappear, and usually for good, the day the decision for divorce is made. *Ms.* Brown is born and she has to begin all over, as though she never existed before, not an unhappy prospect if you think about it.

Do-It-Yourself Divorce

If you are inclined to try it, there is such a thing as do-it-yourself divorce. New York, California and Washington all have provisions for the do-it-yourself route, eliminating the fees for attorneys. This plan can only be used in an uncontested divorce action. It makes no provisions for you to actually go into court and fight it out with your husband. If you go that route, you will definitely need a lawyer, two in fact, one for him and one for you.

Even if your state does not allow do-it-yourself divorce, you can cut your attorney costs considerably by preparing some of the necessary forms, at his direction, and by getting your affairs in total order *before* you visit him. Know when you walk through the attorney's door exactly what you want out of the divorce action. Most lawyers charge by the hour, at least initially. Any time you can save him will in turn save you money.

Things to Settle in the Divorce

When you and your husband or your attorneys sit down to discuss the division of any property, remember to include the following:

Life Insurance. The husband's life insurance policy can be a part of the divorce settlement. He may be directed to leave the proceeds payable in the ex-wife's name or the name of a dependent child of the marriage.

Health Insurance. Courts will, under certain circumstances, direct a husband to continue to carry his children and sometimes even his wife on his health insurance policy. This will save the ex-wife the expense of getting a new policy and cover any unforeseen accidents that may occur. It is a relatively simple task for the husband.

Health Bills. In some cases, if the ex-husband is carrying a dependent child or his ex-wife on his health policy, he may have to be consulted on such expenses as orthodontic work or surgery. A small concession to receive the benefits of his policy.

College Fees. It is possible to include in the divorce settlement a provision for the husband to pay all or a portion of any fees which result when a child enters college. This may also apply to fees paid by the wife if she is endeavoring to learn a trade that she can enter into after graduation, thus relieving some of the financial burden from the ex-husband.

Extra Costs of a Working Mother. A woman who has not been employed before will have to go through the initial expense of clothing and perhaps transportation. It is logical to include a reasonable amount in the divorce agreement to cover this cost since it will cut the woman's earning power considerably in the first months she works. If there are small children involved, babysitting may take up a great deal of her salary. This should be taken into consideration as well, if not in the child support payment then in some other manner.

Moving Costs. If the wife decides to relocate because neither she nor the husband can keep up the house, then her moving expenses should be taken into consideration. Of course, if there are no children involved, the husband will sustain the same expenses moving his belongings and thus the expenses of the two may cancel each other out in terms of who should be compensated. With children, however, it is a different story since the moving will take on much bigger proportions.

Divorce is expensive. There is no way to get around that, but if the marriage is at a standstill then it is the only way and you should take it, whatever the expense. Try to do it with as little dissension as possible. Approach it on an adult level and work out the division of property and all other terms between yourself and your husband. You will save money as well as frayed nerves. If you can't do that, then forge ahead as well as you can and brace yourself for the lawyer's bill. Whatever it is, know that it brings freedom, and whatever the price, it will be worth it.

10

Where to Live

Probably the single most traumatic *and* exciting *and* expensive part of obtaining independence will be the first move . . . getting a place of your own. What you surround yourself with in those first days may mean the difference between happiness and depression. Choose carefully.

How much can you afford? Where do you want to live? Should you consider a permanent move or are you just looking for a place to "put your thoughts together" before you make any major decisions? How much room do you need? Is there only you or are there children to consider?

Make sure that whatever you choose, it is well within your means. If you feel hurried and just do not feel up to searching for the right place immediately, consider the story of a woman we will call Mary. Her life was in a turmoil. She knew she needed to be on her own for a while to find out what, if anything, she valued in life. She wanted a place where she could find herself, a place where she would not be bothered, a place where she would not have to worry about leases, deposits, electricity bills . . . in short, a place where she would have no commitments. She chose a motel in a nearby city. It seemed perfect. For $185 a month and a $60 deposit against phone bills, restaurant and bar tab, she had a telephone, a bed, a maid and no worries about cooking. It was perfect for a while. It gave her time to put things together.

A motel might be a beginning for someone considering changing the status quo, someone who does not really know where she is going. Many women embark on independence after much emotional turmoil; they are hurt and in that hurt, they hide. But you shouldn't hide too long. Nothing is as important as being yourself in a world that accepts you as you are. Motel living is not the best lifestyle. It should be viewed as only a temporary solution while you look for something more suited to your needs and desires. But don't discount the motel because you think you can't afford it. You may see rates like $15 or $30 a night and wonder who could afford that for an extended period of time. However, there are many excellent motels and hotels in the U.S. that offer a monthly rate, the range being somewhere between $150 to $300 a month. When you consider the carefree living involved, it might just be the place you need while you're making up your mind about where you really want to live. But don't be deceived, motel living may be glamorous when you are on vacation but as an everyday experience, it can become depressing very fast, especially when the noises next door are anything but glamorous.

Where to Begin Looking

When the time comes and you are ready to strike out on your own, what will suit your needs best? An apartment, a condominium, a cooperative, a mobile home or a house? What you choose will depend mainly on how much money you have to invest and how permanent you want to get.

Before you make the decision, note the statistics on divorce and marriage. While the divorce rate is nearly 50 percent, the percentage of divorced women in the U.S. is only 3.9 percent. Thus, while you might be in the midst of a divorce or separation now, the odds are that you will remarry. This should be considered in your decision of where to live.

One factor newly independent women have in common is a desire for mobility which is brought about by a constantly changing attitude toward their newly gained independence. They are unsure of themselves, unsure of their directions, and they should stick to the temporary living accommodations. If you have decided where you are going, then perhaps you are ready for a more permanent home.

Where do you start? Most women have not had to actively look for a place to live—at least, not for a long while. And even if they have, in the majority of cases the most recent contact they have had with looking for living quarters has been a home, a home which they cannot now afford on their own. So where do you go from here?

First of all, know that there is a place for you, that there is a place where you can be happy, that you need not depend on someone else to supply you with a roof. Next, consider the options open to you: apartment living, condominiums, cooperatives, mobile homes, and there may even be a house if you are fortunate enough to have saved for the occasion. You can own, rent or lease. You do not have to tie yourself down if you are not yet sure of exactly what you are going to do. And yet if you want permanence, that is there, too. Looking for a place of your own is probably the first step you will take toward your independence. View it as the beginning of an adventure into finding yourself.

Start a check list. What can you afford? If you are thinking of anything but an apartment—a condominium, a cooperative, a mobile home or a house—you will need money for a down payment, closing costs, etc. On top of that, there is maintenance, yearly taxes, and insurance, to mention just a few demands. Of course, there are advantages to owning a home but look at both sides before you decide.

If you are just beginning to be independent, better stick to an apartment. It is likely you will not have a ready reserve of money for the expenses of buying a place, and what little reserve you have, you should not be too inclined to release until you are more sure and secure.

The average American spends some 30 percent of their income acquiring and keeping up their home. That percentage may or may not be right for you. Budget all your expenses before you even begin to look. There is no point in finding the "perfect" home only to be disappointed when you discover you can't afford it. Better to be in a modest but comfortable place with enough money to enjoy your independence.

Apartments

Apartments come in all sizes, varieties and costs. You can rent furnished, unfurnished, with or without club privileges, with or without fireplaces, with or without just about anything. The main considerations are how much room you need and how much you can afford to pay.

A studio apartment may be sufficient if you are alone, but if there are children to consider, you may need a two- or even a three-bedroom apartment. If you have a limited budget, the larger apartments may be a problem to find, but do not despair, there is one somewhere if you look long enough.

Apartment rents can range anywhere from $50 to over $600 for the more luxurious models. You can pay even more than that if you are so inclined. There is an apartment house on Nob Hill in San Francisco that rents some of its more luxurious three-bedroom, unfurnished units for $3000 a month, in New York such places are even higher.

Basically, renting an apartment obligates you in the following ways: (1) Most require a six-month or one-year lease; (2) you must pay a cleaning deposit, usually $50 but in some cases a full month's rent; (3) you might be asked to pay a security deposit, especially if you are renting furnished; (4) you will probably be asked to apply for the apartment, a procedure which involves checking your credit and employment status; (5) animals and children in the apartment may require a breakage fee.

As a guideline, you can assume that it will cost you about two month's rent to get into the apartment if you do not sign a lease. If you do, it will be more like three months' rent. The reason for this is that most leases require you to pay first and last month's rent plus the cleaning deposit and other deposits before occupying. A $200-a-month apartment could, therefore, cost you $600 before you even get to live in it one night. Remember that when you are looking. How much money do you have to get in the door?

Once you have found the place, check it closely . . . the neighbors you will be living with, the noise level of those living around you, the nearest supermarket, the transportation available, the school and playgrounds (if you have children), and any other thing you consider important.

Be sure to read the lease carefully before you sign. Make sure you are getting exactly what you want. If you are really feeling transient, check out the possibility of subleasing (some landlords do not allow it) or cancelling the lease without penalty. Check all the things you feel are important to you *before* you commit yourself. You should not have to worry later about some small item that makes that "perfect" place less perfect than you thought it was.

The Mobile Home

It is estimated that over 8 million Americans are living in mobile homes. It might just be the place for you. Mobile homes are compact, usually mobile and, as a general rule, equipped with everything that you need from the stove to the drapes in the bedroom. Although you can rent them in some parts of the country, mobile homes usually must be purchased. Prices tend to be inexpensive, ranging from $4500 to $30,000. Considering the fact that they are fully furnished, unless otherwise designated, that is cheap by comparison to any other home purchased.

In the mid-seventies, the average mobile home was 12 feet by 60 feet and sold for $7000 furnished. The $30,000 mobile home might be as large as 28 feet by 60 feet and far from mobile. The size and type of mobile home you buy will determine your mobility. The larger ones can be moved but it is difficult and it is best to think of them as permanent structures. If you are really looking for something that you can hook on to and take off cross-country, make sure you are looking at a true *mobile* home. They still do exist and you can still pull them with the family car if you are so inclined.

Assuming that you do not own land, you will have to rent a space to park your home. If you have a definite city in mind, it would be smart to check out the trailer parks for rentals, facilities, and so forth *before* you buy the mobile home.

Park spaces do not usually run any higher than $125 a month and some rents are as low as $30 a month. The average is around $60. There is usually a setup fee tacked on to that first month's rent. Depending on the mobile park's rules, that setup fee can range from $50 to $200. Also many mobile parks require certain modifications to the mobile home to make it more attractive, i.e., skirts to cover the undercarriage, decking at the front and/or back entrance, or canopies. Check these out before you buy the mobile home, if possible, and negotiate to include them in the price of the home itself. If that is not possible, you should check out the costs of these extras before you decide on that park. It might not be worth your while in the long run to buy all those extra decorations just to qualify for a park space.

While you are checking out the park, find out what facilities, if any, are offered for your rent check. Also what services and utilities are included. Who pays water, electricity, garbage and gas? Is a TV cable or antenna hookup available? Is there a swimming pool, laundry, recreation room, a playground or paved walkways? Some mobile parks even go so far as to offer golf courses, fishing ponds, babysitting and clubhouses with planned activities.

If you are considering a permanent location, consider the purchase of a storage shed of your own. They come in all sizes and prices. If you are still in doubt about the mobile park, buy a copy of Woodall's *Mobile Home and Park Directory*. It costs $5.95 and if you cannot find it at the local bookstore, send to Department 240, 500 Hyacinth Place, Highland Park, IL 60035. If your park is listed as "good" in this book, which is revised yearly, you can be assured that it will live up to all your expectations.

Make certain you know exactly what is included in the purchase price. Furniture, carpeting, drapes, lamps and furnace are usually included while such luxuries as dishwasher, garbage disposal, clothes washer and dryer, air conditioning and some types of doors, windows and shutters are not. Know what you are getting for your money before you put it on the line. If you have your own furniture, you may prefer to buy unfurnished. Ask the dealer if that option is available.

Financing Let's say you buy the average mobile home—$7000 furnished, 12 feet by 60 feet. Initial costs will probably run something like this:

20 percent down payment	$1400
Park fee (first and last month's rent)	120
Mobile Park setup	100

If you financed FHA, you would need approximately 20 percent down—in this case $1400. Monthly payments would run about $140 a month including interest. Add that $140 to the cost of renting a park space, $60 average, and you have a total monthly cost of $200 for a home of your own, a home that in five years will belong to you. At the end of that five years, you will no longer have the $140 monthly payment and your home will cost you the meager sum of $60 a month. These monetary rewards over such a short period of time are one of the major reasons that mobile homes are becoming a most popular way to live. In some cases, the down payment may be even less than 20 percent. Depending on the type of financing and the location in the country, it might be as low as 5 percent and the repayment time can range from five to fifteen years.

Under the 1969 Housing Act, the Federal Housing Administration (FHA) can insure mobile homes up to $10,000 and double width homes to $15,000. The 1970 Veterans Housing Act gives VA the power to grant loans up to $10,000 for twelve years and up to $17,500 for fifteen years if a developed lot is included in the price.

Mobile homes are taxable as personal property but this usually does not run more than about $200 for a $10,000 mobile home over a year—far below what the tax on a conventional home can be.

Of course, mobile homes do have disadvantages. To some people they are considered fire hazards. Insurance will cost you much more than it would on an equivalent conventional home. Much of the danger comes from the tight quarters, the minimal number of exits and the quality of the furnace and insulation. To eliminate some of these problems, be sure to insist on proper insulation throughout the home, not only for outside noises but around the furnace area to retard fire spreading should it begin there. Insist on a gun burner furnace. It is far superior and much safer than the obsolete pot burner.

If you set up your mobile home in a windy area, make sure that you follow the manufacturer's recommendations about tiedown. There is some danger of the home blowing over if improperly installed.

One last note, if you should find yourself dissatisfied and unable to get the dealer to repair defects according to the warranty, there is help. Write for a service report from Consumer Action Bureau, Mobile Homes Manufacturers Association, Box 35, Chantilly, VA 22021, or Consumer Affairs Council, Trailer Coach Association, 3855 La Palma Avenue, Anaheim, CA 92806.

The mobile home, while not offering all the answers, does offer one that cannot be totally ignored—the satisfaction of owning your own home at a relatively low price.

A Cooperative or Condominium?

If you are a confirmed apartment dweller, if you prefer the convenience of owning your own home without having to worry about outside upkeep, if you want those "extra" conveniences like a swimming pool, sauna, etc., then perhaps the answer for you is the cooperative or condominium.

More and more people are turning to cooperatives and particularly condominiums as a means of investing money that would otherwise be "thrown away" on monthly rent. Both types of dwellings enable you to deduct interest and taxes on your yearly tax statement, a benefit not to be looked at lightly.

Basically, both cooperatives and condominiums are the same: apartments for sale. One out of every seven apartments built today is a condominium or a cooperative apartment, and prices have skyrocketed with the increased interest in purchasing by the American homeowner. Prices can range into the $100,000 figure and the average price today runs as high as $40,000.

The Cooperative   When you put your money in a cooperative, you do not buy an apartment, rather you buy shares in the cooperative. Let's say you want a two-bedroom, two-bath apartment. For the sake of an example, let's say that your purchase price is $35,000 and for that $35,000 you get ten shares in the cooperative. As a point of comparison, someone who bought a three-bedroom, two-bath apartment in the same building for $45,000 gets fifteen shares in the cooperative. How many shares you acquire depends on the size and purchase price of the apartment you choose.

Actually what you are doing when you buy into a cooperative is buying a building with others. Say there are ten apartments in the building. If all are sold, the building has ten owners, and you are one. How much you own of the building depends on the size and price of the apartment you purchased. The tenant who paid more will have the greater interest. None, however, will have a controlling interest. You are, in essence, all equal. As owners of the building, each of you must contribute to a maintenance fee from which the property taxes and general upkeep of the building are taken. How much you pay into this maintenance fee depends on the money needed for that purpose. If it is, say, $2500 a year, you share would be a portion of that amount, dependent on the size of your share in the cooperative. The tenant with a bigger share would pay more.

Remember, however, that upkeep costs for the building and property taxes have a way of going up. As that happens, your maintenance fee will increase proportionally.

It is cheaper to own a cooperative than it is to rent, an estimated 20 percent cheaper. You may deduct that portion of the maintenance fee that goes for mortgage interest on the land and property taxes from your income tax. And, of course, you may deduct any interest paid by you on money borrowed to purchase shares in the cooperative.

Before you commit yourself to a cooperative, check the local lending institutions. Many will not lend as much as they would on a condominium or a house. The percentage could be as low as 50 or even lower. Of course, the lower the percentage the higher will be your down payment. Interest rates may also be higher on money borrowed, as much as two percent higher. That can amount to a considerable sum over an extended period of time.

As a cooperative owner, you have a say in the disposition of the building. Decisions on upkeep, remodeling or additions are decided by *all* the owners. In essence, the building and the apartment, and all the extras such as swimming pool, sauna, laundry room, belong to you.

If the value of the cooperative rises, the value of your apartment rises, as a general rule. There are some cooperatives, however, that require you to sell your apartment back to the cooperative for the same price you originally paid for it should you decide to leave. Thus, you only gain the savings you have made on your income tax through interest and taxes paid on the apartment. This is one point that you should check before you move in.

What holds true for the rise in value of your cooperative, also holds true if the value declines. You may lose money. So you must weigh the alternative of renting against purchasing. One of the major disadvantages of buying a cooperative is the fact that as a shareholder in the building you must make up the deficit if someone defaults on payment. If, for example, the tenant with the $45,000 apartment loses his job and can no longer make the monthly payments, his portion of the mortgage on the building and land falls to the remaining tenants and each of them must share in his payment. This also is true if the cooperative is not completely sold. A new cooperative with twenty apartments is built. A month after it opens it is half sold and the city announces that a new freeway is going in right next to it. The news panics potential buyers and, after a year, it is still only partially sold. You, as one of the first buyers, must carry the burden of those apartments still empty. This is rather an extreme illustration but demonstrates the point.

Sometimes you cannot sell or sublet your apartment without the approval of the other owners. This approval may, if times are hard, be difficult to get if you wish to sell. By the same token, they may refuse to let you sublet in order "to keep up the quality of the tenants." (Those who own usually put much more into keeping up an apartment than those who are just renting.)

The key to buying a cooperative is "read the small print and know exactly what you are getting for your money." Owning a cooperative can be to your advantage but you should be aware of the pitfalls.

Condominiums Unlike the cooperative, buying a condominium is buying an apartment. You are legally the owner of "your" apartment, the space you actually occupy. You are responsible for your own property taxes and your own mortgage payment. What happens to the other tenants in the condominium will not affect that payment. Of course should a number of tenants default, the condominium's stability will be questioned and the value of your unit will fall accordingly.

You are substantially, however, "your own boss" and can pretty much do as you please with your apartment. Renting out your unit is easier in most cases, although this is a point you should check before signing the agreement, or covenant which many places insist upon. Some of the condominiums in resort areas, in fact, offer a rental service for a percentage of the rental price. The percentage is quite often high and, although you may realize some profit from doing this, you will not realize a great deal. For that reason, it is not an income you should count on when considering the purchase of a resort unit.

Like the cooperative, you agree to pay a maintenance fee for the upkeep of the building and grounds. Usually, the fee is much lower than that required by the cooperative. If it seems too low, however, particularly on a new condominium, check it out. It may be that the developer is undercutting the maintenance fee until after all the units are sold. Once full occupancy is reached, the fee is likely to skyrocket.

Financing your condominium may be fairly easy. Both FHA

and VA will back mortgages on condominiums. Obtaining the necessary funds will probably be no more painful than obtaining them for a comparable house. The same rules apply regarding financing, i.e., percentage down payment, terms and length of mortgage.

Provided the condominium does not decrease in value, you will have no difficulty in selling it if you desire. They are in great demand at present and with the increasing population and decreasing proportionate land available, their popularity is not expected to decline in the near future.

As a tenant, you are a member of the tenants' organization. As such, you determine the maintenance required for the grounds and any "extras" the condominium might offer, such as swimming pool, marina, golf course, sauna, and so on. Thus you have a say in any additional funds spent and will be more inclined to accept any resulting increase in your portion of the maintenance fee.

One major pitfall to check when buying a condominium is whether or not you are also buying the land. Some of the condominiums on the market sell only the apartment. The buyer must lease the land from the developer for, say, $500 a year. Admittedly, the sum might be small but the aggravation may be extreme if you think you have bought both apartment and land only to discover that you are still paying rent on the land. A disaster that might grow out of this oversight on your part may be the loss of your apartment. The developer may lease the land to the owners' association for, say, fifty years. At the end of that time, he may decide that the complex needs renovating and proceed to tear down the existing buildings. The land is his and he has every right to do so. There are no provisions for tenants who might own the condominiums. They are, as the saying goes, "out of luck" . . . also money and home. It is imperative that you know exactly where you stand or on what your apartment stands. Does it belong to you or doesn't it? This might be one of your considerations when making the initial purchase. If you do not own the land, how long is the leasehold arrangement? How will it affect you when it expires?

Like buying a house, buying a condominium does have the benefits of writing off a portion of your payment on your tax return. You build equity and, provided the unit does not decrease in value, you may realize a profit when you sell. You are realizing dollar savings not paper savings (piling up of cancelled checks) as you do when renting.

Also like buying a house, buying a condominium or a cooperative should be done with care. If you are unsure of yourself, if you do not know all the pitfalls to look for, if the small print is too filled with legal jargon to mean anything to you, then by all means, consult a lawyer. His fee will, in the long run, be well worth the peace of mind and absence of later legal hassles.

Where to Live–A House of Your Own

Some people, especially women, just will not consider buying a house. The commitment to long-term mortgages, continual upkeep and property taxes scares them off. Many of them have a right to be scared. Down payments, closing costs, points, insurance, county taxes, interest charges, 30-year notes, all coupled with a bathroom that will not function properly, a roof that leaks and a kitchen sink that is perpetually stopped up, are enough to scare anyone off. However, if your income is such that you can manage the costs, in these inflationary times it can be a good investment. Take your chances and hedge your bet with expert advice from a lawyer and help from a wise real estate agent.

If you are seriously considering buying a home, now may be the time to check into it. What with inflation and increased population, home values in the mid-seventies have been increasing at the rate of 1 percent a *month*. Only a few short years ago, it was 1 percent a *year*. With statistics like that, owning your own home becomes not only a necessary investment for tax benefits but one that is virtually guaranteed to reap "big" rewards. As a matter of fact, at the current rate of increase in home values, your home could double its value in seven years' time.

What to Look For   Buying a house is probably the single largest expense you will incur during your lifetime. For that reason, if for no other, you should be aware of all the contingencies involved in the purchase of a house—everything from the condition of the oven to the cost of the loan to the way your neighbors keep up their houses. All these will reflect on your home in some way.

Start your search by analyzing your own needs. Why do you

want or need a house? Is it really economically feasible for you to own a house? For your own peace of mind after you have signed on the dotted line, ask yourself these questions now:

1. How much space do you need? Would an apartment or a condominium answer your needs just as well? Are you looking for a one-bedroom or a four-bedroom home? Do you need all that room? Remember you are going to have to clean it. If you are alone, you could spend your spare time doing nothing but cleaning.

2. What is your income? Can you afford to purchase a home? Check out the actual cost of buying a house: the monthly payment, taxes, interest payments, upkeep, and so forth. Will you be able to keep up with the costs of owning your own home? Remember, mortgage payments, like rent, do go up.

3. The single biggest advantage to buying a house will be the tax benefits you will get from the interest you will be paying on your mortgage. These interest payments can run as high as $2000 or even $10,000 a year or more. Every penny you pay in interest can be deducted when filing your personal income tax, a benefit not afforded you with rent payments.

4. Are you stable enough to buy a home? Do you plan to move within the next six years? Statistics tell us that in order to make anything on the purchase of a house, you must spend at least six years living there. Of course, any profits you reap are dependent on the value of the house rising within that time. Nothing says that will definitely happen. The value may fall and you will lose money. The odds, however, are in your favor. If you don't feel certain that you'll be in an area for some time, then don't buy a house. Rent, instead. Buying will only tie you down, something you will not want if you are undecided about your future.

5. Who is going to cut the lawn? How much yard work does the house have? Can you afford to hire someone to help you? If not, are you prepared to spend many of your weekends pulling weeds, cutting the grass and trimming the trees?

6. How much money do you have available for a down payment? The average house costs $30,000 these days. If you get a conventional loan, you will need a 20 percent down payment. That's $6000. Do you have it? Can you get it? If not, you are not ready to buy. You could arrange for a "second" with the seller.

That means that you borrow a portion of the $6000 from him. You promise to pay him back in five years (that is the customary time limit). This means an additional monthly payment and a balloon payment at the end of five years. A second is a way to meet the down payment but it means going into debt even more. Is that what you want?

7. Do you have an extra slush fund for closing costs and other fees that will come up during the purchase? These costs may run as high as $1500 on the average house. This is in addition to the down payment. Do you have enough money available to cover them?

There is even more to be considered. Buying a house is not all "peaches and cream." As a matter of fact, it may seem at times like the dumbest thing you ever did. If you have the funds to back you, however, and you really want a house, in the long run it can be worthwhile both from the standpoint of having a place of your own and the security of having invested your money wisely. There are no sure investments in this world but putting your money into property is as close as you can come.

Expenses Before you leap into the purchase of a house, consider those extra expenses that a house will mean to your monthly budget. They could be considerable, and they will not be a part of your mortgage payment. These will have to come out of your daily expense budget.

1. *Water.* If you have been an apartment dweller, you most likely have not been paying for water as a separate expense. It was included in your rent. When you own your own house, you will pay for water. Depending on the size of the house, it could run from $10 to $20 a month.

2. *Garbage.* Once again, an expense that an apartment dweller never has but a homeowner does. It will run you approximately $4 a month.

3. *Electricity.* You will have, no doubt, paid electricity in an apartment but a house generally requires more electricity. Expect your electricity bill to go up in proportion to the increased amount of space you will have in a house. An average three-bedroom house can use $60 in electricity and gas each month while a two-bedroom house may use $50.

These are only three extra expenses you will feel immediately on moving into a house. They are not, by any means, the only ones. To these you can add painting, plumbing, appliance repair, lawn care and outside upkeep of the house. All of these things you have never had to worry about if you have always lived in an apartment. Now they will be your responsibility.

Finding a Real Estate Broker

If you are going to buy, you need a real estate broker to help you find the perfect place at the perfect price to fit your budget. You will not be committing yourself to buy by calling a broker. You will just be expressing interest. You can look at houses for weeks, months even, provided the broker will continue to show them to you. It will not cost you a penny. The broker costs you money only when you sign on the dotted line to buy a house. If you don't buy you will never pay a cent for the services. Even when you do buy you are not billed directly. The broker collects a percentage (usually 6%) of the selling price of the house. It is likely that the price you pay for the house is proportionately higher than if you had bought directly from the owner but the expert advice gained in using a broker is well worth the additional cost.

The point is, do not worry about what the broker costs you. Rather, devote yourself to finding a good broker, one you can trust. If you know a broker from past experience, all the better. If not, maybe a close friend recently bought a house. Ask who her broker was. If the broker is not in your area, maybe she can suggest one who is. Or ask your banker for the name of a good broker. Banks deal with real estate brokers all the time.

How to Remember the Houses You See   You will probably look at a dozen or more homes before you settle on one. You may never find the right one. You may look for months on end or you may find everything you want in the very first one you see. Obviously, if you look at more than one, you will forget the benefits of one house over another as you jump from one to another. In this way, you may let the right house slip by only because you saw it a week ago, not yesterday. This problem can be solved by your real estate broker. He will have a "listing card" on each house he shows you. On the card are all the specifics of the house—size, age, features inside and out—and it also has an outside picture of the house. To help you remember the inside, you might take along a Polaroid camera on your daily house hunts. Take shots of the areas most important to you. In the privacy of your home, you can scan them and study the benefits of the house at your leisure without the pressures of the real estate broker at your arm.

Finding Your Dream House

When you are looking for a house, there are many things to consider. On first glance, it may appear to be just what you have always wanted. At second glance, it may reveal peeling paint on the exterior or plumbing that has a history of backing up or wiring that will not accommodate a clothes dryer. You must learn to look beyond the facade the seller has put up for you. Remember when he goes, nearly everything that is not nailed down in the house will go with him. You are not interested in the way he has it furnished. What you should be concerned with are the walls, the pipes, the built-in appliances, the paint, the sewer, the lawn—all these and more are what will make your life in the house either a dream or a nightmare.

A Check List   Add any other items you feel concerned about in a house.

1. *Heating and air conditioning.* What does the home have to offer in these two items? Are they sufficient to heat and/or cool the house? Are they in good working order? How old are they? If they are fairly old, when was the last time they were checked, cleaned or otherwise serviced?

2. *Plumbing.* This is almost impossible to test before moving in. You can do things like turning on several faucets at once to see if the water pressure is affected. You can also check the exposed pipes. Are they rusted or corroded in any way? Any major difficulties in plumbing will probably not be discovered until after you buy the house. For example, the first house I bought had a problem with clogged pipes. The former owner was a masonry worker and the residue from his work clothes had, over the years, settled in the pipes. As a result, every time I washed clothes, the water backed up in one of the bathrooms. The pipe going into the sewer was so clogged that it could not handle a major influx of water such as a draining washing machine. The only way to remedy this was to have the pipe

cleaned out by a plumber, an expensive proposition.

3. *Drapes*. As a general rule, the drapes stay with the house. However, do not assume this. Make it a part of the agreement. Buying new drapes could cost you as much as $100 a window.

4. *Light fixtures*. Do the light fixtures stay? Many of the recently built homes do not have overhead light fixtures. Lighting is dependent on hanging lamps that are independent of the structure. If you do not include these in the agreement, you may find yourself with a beautiful house but no light. The seller will pack them along with the dishes.

5. *Carpeting*. Check for wear. Ask when it was put in. If you feel it needs to be replaced, bring it up with the real estate broker. Maybe he can get an allowance from the seller on the price of the house.

6. *Roof*. Find out if the roof leaks. The seller probably will not tell you, but with a careful eye you can find out for yourself. Look at the ceiling inside for water spots. Check the walls. The seller may be able to mask some of these but he will probably not get them all. Look outside at the roof. The edges of it can tell you a lot. The cost of a roofing job can run into the thousands, not a happy prospect for the new homeowner.

7. *Finishing*. Check under furniture. The seller may be hiding something under that beautiful couch. When I bought my first home, one of the rooms was a lovely little family room that the seller had added to the house. The fireplace was roaring and his wife and children were curled up on a lovely couch watching television. The setting was great and I fell for it. After I signed the papers and he moved out, I went again to look at the house. The family room was still there; the fireplace was still there; the couch was gone, and underneath where it once stood was bare concrete. The carpeting did not cover that part of the room. Furthermore, the wall from the bottom of the sliding door to the floor of the room (some two feet) was also raw concrete. The steps that were once there were ripped out and the area never completed. My family room was not what it had seemed to be. Don't let it happen to you.

8. *Sewer system*. Some houses still have their own sewer systems; they are not hooked up to the city's. If the house has this type of sewer system, ask when it was cleaned last. When

will it need to be cleaned again? How much will it cost you?

9. *Electrical wiring*. Is the electrical wiring in the house sufficient for your needs? Some of the older homes may not have the wiring required for your clothes dryer or there may not be enough power for you to run a color TV set and the dryer at the same time. To avoid future hassles caused by blown fuses, find out now what the wiring in the house can handle.

10. *Termites*. Little bugs that eat up your house. Generally, these are no problems for the homeowner. The law requires a termite inspection and if any are found the seller must exterminate them and repair any damage.

11. *Bathroom flooring*. One of the most vulnerable places in any house is the bathroom flooring. Poor tiling, sinks running over onto the floor and plugged toilets can cause the floor to rot. It can be happening without your even knowing. Do not buy a house with it already in progress. Check for any decay in the wood flooring. If there is carpeting on the floor, pull it up and look underneath. Is the wood warping? If it is, it means that it has been exposed to repeated soaking with water. It may mean that the toilet is prone to overflow. The floor can tell you a lot.

12. *Paint—inside and out*. Is it peeling? Will you need to repaint soon? If so, find out how much it will cost you. Call a house painter and check it out. If this is a factor in your purchase, tell the real estate broker; maybe he can get the seller to come down to accommodate this cost.

13. *The lawn*. Has it been well cared for or does it require reseeding? Is it full of weeds? Will you need to put a lot of money and work into it? Will you have the time or will you have to hire someone to do it for you? You can check with a local yard service or gardener to find out how much it will cost you to have it done.

14. *Kitchen appliances*. Does the garbage disposal work? How old is the stove, the dishwasher? Will you need to replace them soon? Do all the appliances in the kitchen work? Check them out. A new oven can cost you a bundle.

There are many more things you will want to check. For more help, write for a free booklet: *Basic Housing Inspection*, U.S. Department of Health, Education and Welfare, Room 1587, Parklawn Building, 5600 Fishers Lane, Rockville, MD 20852.

Financing

You have it. Your perfect house. Now is the time to consider the price more carefully. Can you afford it? Remember the total price will affect the down payment, the monthly payments, the property taxes and the expenses of keeping it in good running order.

Ask your real estate broker to work up costs for you before you sign. How much will it cost you to buy this house, including closing costs, down payment and the other expenses? How much will the property taxes run? Can they be included in your monthly payment? What expenses will you have to make immediately to keep the house in good condition? Where can you get a loan?

Loans and Interest   Your real estate broker should be able to direct you to the commercial bank, mortgage company or savings and loan association with the loan program best suited to your individual needs. He should also be able to tell you where the cheapest rates can be found at any given time, and with the radical fluctuation of interest rates now, this can mean a substantial amount of money to you.

The most common type of home loan is called a conventional loan with terms of 20 percent down on an 80 percent loan appraised on the basis of a thirty-year mortgage at the current interest rate. Veterans can take advantage of a VA loan which requires nothing down on a loan up to $70,000. While seemingly a "good deal" on the surface, you should keep in mind that the more you borrow, the higher the monthly payment. Be sure to check out the monthly payment figure.

The greatest influence on your monthly payment, whatever type of loan you decide on, will be the interest rate. To get some idea of what is happening to interest rates, consider the following: According to figures from the Bank of America, the interest rate on a thirty-year conventional loan at the beginning of 1974 was 8½ percent. By April, 1974, it had risen to 9¼ percent. In September, it reached a high of 10½ percent on a 66⅔ percent loan over a thirty-year period. At that time, Bank of America was not even offering the 80 percent, thirty-year loan. Other banks, mortgage and savings and loan associations were—at a high of 11½ percent interest. In 1975, the interest rate began to drop rapidly and in April 1975, it was back to a low of 8¾ percent. However, in May, the rate was already climbing again to 9 percent.

Understand that even a ½ percent interest increase can mean thousands of dollars in interest to you when considered over a thirty-year period. You could end up paying for your house three times over if the interest rate is extraordinarily high. By any means, there is hardly any way, short of paying cash, that you can get around paying for it at least twice. It is a sad fact of house buying. Let your real estate broker be your guide when looking for the lowest interest rate. He will know what is available.

Closing Costs Once you have found financing, you will run across extra expenses that must come out of your pocket. These are called closing costs. Included in these costs will be title search, appraisal fees, points charged by the lender, insurance, and so on. Probably the most mysterious of these costs will be those called *points*. Actually, there is nothing mysterious about them. A point is nothing more than extra money you pay the lender for the money to buy the house. It is one one-hundredth of the total amount of the mortgage loan. If the loan is $24,000, one point is $240. If the lender charges you three points for the mortgage, he is charging you $720. This is an expense that you will pay in the closing costs; you cannot add it to the loan itself. Although points may seem illegal, they are not. Points are an accepted practice by all lenders. The number of points a lender is going to charge you should be a consideration as well as the interest rate.

For the purpose of estimating your closing costs, use the following check list. Get the actual costs from your real estate broker or the lending firm.

Policy title insurance and escrow costs
Recording of deed and trust deed
Points
Appraisal fee
Tax service
Credit report
Interest per day on your loan from the close of escrow to 30 days before the first payment
Proration of taxes (that amount of taxes you will be responsible for paying in the next tax bill)
Fire insurance

Life insurance on buyer (to pay for the house in the event of your
death)

These are not necessarily all the closing costs but at least the
list will get you started. Go over it with your real estate broker.
Ask his assistance in adding other costs you might or might not
expect.

Before You Sign Haggle. Never accept the seller's price as
your price. You can generally get the house for thousands of
dollars less. The seller always asks more for the house than he
expects to get. He plans to come down on the price. Make him.

Although the interest rate should definitely have some bearing
on whether you buy, you should also consider the effect of a
delay on the value of the house. With home values rising at a rate
of 1 percent a month in the seventies, you may find that a high
interest rate might be preferable to waiting for a while and then
paying an even higher price for the house. For example, a house
selling for $50,000 in July 1974, might break down this way: 80
percent loan, thirty years, 11¾ percent interest, $403.77 monthly
payment (principal and interest only), $10,000 down payment.
The same house could have sold for $57,500 in April 1975, with
the following loan changes: 80 percent loan, thirty years, 8¾
percent interest, $361.90 monthly payment, $11,500 down payment. Although the monthly payment may be more should you
buy at the higher interest rate rather than waiting (assuming the
rates will drop), consider the additional $1,500 needed for the
loan down payment and the extra $6,000 added to the thirty-year
loan, not to mention the fact that you have paid almost a year of
rent. Also these figures assume that the interest rate will decrease over a period of time, an assumption which, of course, is
not necessarily true. Talk to some of the "old timers" who can
remember the days of 5 percent interest rates. You will find they
are not really that old.

What it all comes down to is this—if you are going to buy, you
might as well buy now no matter what the interest rates are. It is
difficult to predict what will happen to interest rates over a
period of time, but you can be certain that if conditions remain
the same in the housing market (and there is no reason to believe
they will not), the cost of the house will definitely increase.

11

Free Insurance Against the Unexpected–Government Programs

Most of us feel that disaster always happens to the "other guy," which leaves us vulnerable and not prepared should it happen "here," to one of us—to you. What do you do when you lose your job with no money in the bank and a stack of bills on your kitchen table? What do you do when you can't find another job and there is no food in the house? Where can you turn if you are injured in an automobile accident with no insurance to cover your medical expenses? If the accident leaves you unable to work, what then? If you are totally disabled, what can you do?

If you have left yourself totally unprepared, you may deserve some moments of anxiety, but don't despair, there are government and state "insurance policies" that everyone is entitled to. You will not get rich off them. As a matter of fact, you will probably have to lower your standard of living, but at least you will be able to live until you get back on your feet.

Some look on this type of money as charity. It is not. All are programs that you and/or members of your family have helped to support over the years with your taxes. It is only right that you should get a return on that investment when you need it most. After all, in a sense, it is your money.

Social Security/Disability Insurance

Most people think of social security as old-age pensions. It is more than that. Social Security also provides benefits to the disabled and the dependents of the disabled. If you have been employed and a paying member of Social Security, you are eligible for these benefits.

To qualify, you must fulfill the following requirements:

1. If you are above the age of thirty-one, you must have worked and paid into Social Security half the quarters during the ten years

immediately prior to the disability. This is roughly equivalent to five years. If you are under thirty-one, you must have worked in at least half of the quarters from age twenty-one to your present age. The minimum is six quarters.

2. You must be disabled for at least six months before you receive the first disability payment and you must expect to be disabled for at least one year. This waiting period assumes that you have medical insurance and other compensation to cover you until that time.

How much will you receive? The average payment is 60 percent of your take-home pay when you were working. If you have dependent children, Social Security will also pay them in addition to what you receive. Age limit for these dependents is eighteen unless they are full-time students, then the limit goes to twenty-two. If you are permanently disabled but decide to go back to work, you can still receive these benefits up to a specified period of time. For nine months after you return to the job, you may receive disability with the assumption that this is a trial period. If you continue to work after the nine months, the payments continue for another three months until you are considered totally adjusted to your disability as it affects your job. After that, payments cease. If you are permanently disabled, whether you continue to stay at home or require professional attention in a nursing home, disability payments will continue indefinitely.

For additional information, contact your local Social Security Office. You will find it listed in the telephone book under U.S. Government.

State Disability Insurance

All states now have some form of disability insurance. Requirements for receiving these benefits are generally the same as that for Social Security. Check with your state Welfare Department (sometimes called Social Services Department) for information regarding the benefits available to you under your state program.

Medicare

You do not have to be old to receive Medicare. Like Social Security, you can receive benefits if you become disabled. Requirements for receiving Medicare before the age of sixty-five hinge on your ability to qualify for Social Security. If you are entitled to at least twenty-four consecutive months of payments from Social Security Disability Insurance, then you may receive Medicare benefits in the twenty-fifth month. Your Social Security office will notify you that you are eligible for Medicare. These benefits include hospital and, if you elect, medical (doctor-related bills). The small premium you are charged for these benefits will be deducted from your Social Security Disability check.

How much coverage do you receive? All or part of hospital, nursing, doctor's bills, outpatient hospital services, physical therapy, speech pathology services, X-rays, radiation treatments, rental and purchase of equipment, supplies used for dressing wounds, and artificial limbs and eyes. There are more. Some of the things you will not be covered for include drugs not hospital-related, routine examinations whether it be a dental check, a testing of your eyes or a physical exam, hearing aids, false teeth, orthopedic shoes, to name just a few.

Whatever your age, you can receive full Medicare benefits if you suffer from chronic kidney disease which requires kidney dialysis or makes it necessary for you to undergo a kidney operation.

If you do become disabled, check into your rights under Medicare. Laws are always changing and it is possible that you could be eligible sooner or for more coverage than is stipulated here.

State Medical Insurance

Many states have some type of medical insurance available for those unable to pay. Qualifications tend to be the same as with Medicare. Check with your state Welfare Department.

Unemployment Benefits

If you lose your job, you are entitled to unemployment benefits, provided you are actively seeking but cannot find another job. Unemployment benefits are based on your income for a specific period of time immediately prior to your leaving your job. Benefits can range from $5 to $150 a week. The law stipulates that you can receive these benefits for twenty-six weeks; however, the high rate of unemployment has prompted states to stretch this to thirty-nine weeks. In some cases, you can get an extension on that.

The one main provision of receiving unemployment insurance is that you must be actively seeking employment. You must undergo interviews with the state employment service and be available to go out on job interviews should this agency find a job suitable to your talents and skills. Unemployment insurance is not a free ride. It is a right you have paid for and one you deserve while you look for another job. Do not be ashamed to apply for it.

In most states, there is a waiting period before you can receive the first check. It is important, therefore, that you apply for unemployment immediately, even if you think you will be able to get another job easily. The waiting period is usually two weeks and there is always the chance you will not find a job before then. It doesn't hurt to be safe.

Should you find a job, simply notify the state employment center (it may be called another name in your state). They will close the file. It's as simple as that.

Food Stamps

The Food Stamp Program was set up to enable low-income families to buy a greater variety of food to improve diets. Divorced or single women, with their low incomes, will probably be able to qualify for these. The U.S. Department of Agriculture sponsors the program. It is administered, however, through state Welfare Departments.

To purchase food stamps, you must (1) have no job, (2) have only a part-time job, (3) not earn much money, (4) be on public welfare or (5) be on Social Security or a small pension.

How much you pay for food stamps depends on how much money you make and the size of the household. The idea behind food stamps is, in essence, to enable those who qualify to purchase $25 worth of groceries for only $20—you give the Welfare Department $20 and they give you $25 in grocery stamps. The actual ratio of what you pay to the value of the stamps varies according to your situation. Food stamps can be purchased at some banks and post offices once you obtain the necessary eligibility card from the Welfare Department. This card indicates how many and at what price you may purchase the stamps.

There is a thirty-day waiting period for food stamps, unless you can prove urgency. In that case, you may be able to get stamps the day you apply. When you apply for food stamps, you will need the following documents:

(1) address of household
(2) number in household
(3) the income of the household substantiated by paycheck receipts
(4) rent receipts
(5) doctor bills being paid

In order to receive food stamps, you must be actively pursuing work if you are not employed. The requirements say that you must be interviewed by the state employment office as with unemployment insurance.

For further information on the Food Stamp Program, write for the pamphlet "The Food Stamp Program," U.S. Department of Agriculture, Food and Nutrition Service, Washington, DC. Your state Welfare Department will also provide you with additional information.

Epilogue

On Your Own With Your Finances on the Plus Side

Becoming financially independent need not be a process of becoming totally independent. It does not mean that you have to shut yourself off from the world or from a man. Becoming financially independent means becoming secure in yourself, knowing that you can make it on your own.

A woman no longer rests on the pedestal once built for her by her man. She is no longer content to rest there, dormant—awakening only at his call. She has long fought for her freedom from that pedestal and has won it more times than she has lost. If she is still there it is because she continually sees herself in that role and flings herself back up there expecting the reverent care that she once enjoyed.

Today, however, few men see her in that role. She has become through her own fight for freedom a person, not a goddess to be worshipped. Today a woman must be able to make it on her own in this world and it is not a kind world. She must know not only what to do but when to do it and often who to do it to. She cannot trust in others to take care of her. She must learn to take care of herself.

Resources

General Reading

Auerbach, Sylvia. *Your Money: How To Make It Stretch*. New York: Doubleday, 1974.

Black, Joan. *The Modern Woman's Key To Financial Security*. California: Major, 1975.

Cowan, Ronnie. "Doris Day: My Most Costly Mistake As a Wife." *Ladies' Home Journal*, January 1973.

Day, Doris. *Doris Day: Her Own Story,* as told to A. E. Hotchner. New York: Morrow, 1976.

DeCrow, Karen. *Sexist Justice*. New York: Vintage Books, 1974.

Dorfman, John. *Consumer Survival Kit*. New York: Praeger Publishers, 1975.

Grimstad, Kirsten & Rennie, Susan, editors. *The New Woman's Survival Sourcebook*. New York: Alfred A. Knopf, Inc., 1975.

Halcomb, Ruth. *Money & The Working Ms*. California: Books for Better Living, 1974.

"Money", *Ms. Magazine*, September, 1974. 114+.

Porter, Sylvia. *Money Book*. New York: Doubleday & Co., Inc., 1975.

Simons, Gustave. *What Every Woman Doesn't Know*. New York: Macmillan, 1964.

Sweeney, Karen O'Connor. *Every Woman's Guide to Family Finances*. California: Major Books, 1976.

The Law—Your Rights

Boyer, Gene. *Are Women Equal Under the Law?* Wisconsin: Beaver Dam, 1971.

Brooks, Thomas R. "At Last: Fair Credit Treatment for Women," *Reader's Digest,* September, 1975, 19–24.

Brown, Barbara, Thomas Emerson, Ann Freedman. "The Equal Rights Amendment, A Constitutional Basis for Equal Rights for

Women," From the *Yale Law Journal*, 401 A Yale Station, New Haven, Conn. 06520. $3.50.

Cotte, Anna and Tess Gill. *Women's Rights: A Practical Guide*, Canada: Penguin Books Canada Ltd., 1975.

DeCrow, Karen. *Sexist Justice, How Legal Sexism Affects You*, New York: Vintage Books, 1975.

"The ERA: What It Means To Men and Women". From the League of Women Voters, 1730 M Street, NW, Washington, D. C. 20036. $3/one hundred pamphlets.

"Fed Issues Equal Credit Rules." *San Francisco Chronicle*, October 17, 1975.

Gager, Nancy, editor. *Women's Rights Almanac*, published yearly. New York: Harper & Row.

"The Geography of Inequality—Women's Legal Rights in 50 States". *McCall's Magazine*, February, 1971.

"A Guide to Federal Laws Prohibiting Sex Discrimination". U. S. Commission on Civil Rights. Write to: Superintendent of Documents, U. S. Government Printing Office, Washington, D.C. 20402. $1.40.

Mercer, Marilyn. "ERA: What Would It Really Mean?" *McCall's Magazine*, July, 1976, 107+.

"Women and Credit—What the New Law Means". *San Francisco Chronicle*, October 27, 1975.

"Women Move Toward Credit Equality, Equal Credit Opportunity Act". *Time*, October 27, 1975, 63–4.

How To Get Credit

"Credit for Women", a pamphlet. Write to Consumer Credit Association, P. O. Box 2049, Dallas, Texas 75221. $.25.

"The Credit Game—Unfair to Women?" *McCall's Magazine*, September, 1972, 29+.

"Credit Unions: What They Are, How They Operate, How to Join, How to Start One." 1973. Write to: Credit Union National Association, Inc., P. O. Box 431, Madison, Wisconsin 53701.

"F.H.A. Mortgages". Write to: Federal Housing Administration, Department of Housing and Urban Development, 451 7th St., S. W., Washington D.C. 20410.

Feminist Credit Unions. Refer to Savings Chapters for addresses.

"Giving Women Credit". *New Republic*, August 11, 1973, 9.

"How To Establish Credit". Write to: Bank of America, Box 37128, San Francisco, Calif. 94137.

"How To Shop For Credit". *Consumer Republic*, March, 1975, 171–8.

National Organization for Women (NOW). Check your telephone book for local chapter.

Rupen, Alice and Candace Wiad. *Source Materials on Women and Credit: An Annotated Bibliography,* Washington D. C. Center for Women Policy Studies, 1974. Available for $1 from the Center for Women Policy Studies, Room 508, 2000 P St., N.W., Washington, D.C. 20036.

"Women and Credit", National Organization for Women, National Office, New York, New York. $3 members/$5 non-members.

"Women and Credit", National Organization for Women, San Francisco Chapter, P. O. Box 1267, San Francisco, Calif. 94101.

"A Women's Bank in San Francisco". *San Francisco Chronicle,* January 22, 1976.

"A Women's Bank Opens". *San Francisco Chronicle,* October 17, 1975.

"Women Move Toward Credit Equality, Equal Credit Opportunity Act", *Time,* October 27, 1975, 63–4.

"Women Win More Credit". *Business Week,* January 12, 1974, 76–8.

"You've Gotta Give Her Credit". Printed by the California Commission on the Status of Women, 926 J St., Room 1003, Sacramento, Calif. 95814. 1975. A sample of the type of material you can expect to obtain from the Commission on the Status of Women in your state.

Budgeting

"Do You Keep a Budget?" *Home and Garden,* April, 1976, 109–110.

"Good Basic Ways to Set Up a Budget". *Good Housekeeping,* November, 1974, 236.

"Make a New Budget For Times Like This". *Changing Times,* May, 1975, 6–11.

"Making the Most of Your Money". 1974. Write to Education Services, Institute of Life Insurance, 277 Park Ave., New York 10017.

"Managing Money: When a Woman Finds She's On Her Own". An interview. *U. S. News,* May 20, 1974, 75–7.

"Step by Step To Money Management". Write to Consumer & Community Services, Institute of Life Insurance, 277 Park Ave., New York, 10017.

Savings

Feminist Credit Unions. All credit unions will gladly supply you with not only printed matter on savings but guidance. Check address of the Feminist Credit Union nearest you. Address in Savings Chapter.

Oliver, J., "You Have a Friend: Feminist Credit Unions". *Ms. Magazine,* January, 1975, 21.

"Ways to Save Your Money". Consumer Information Report #2, Bank of America. Write to Bank of America, Box 37128, San Francisco 94137.

Insurance

"The Booklet You Have In Your Hand Is Not Designed To Sell You Life Insurance". 1974. Write to Consumer and Community Services, Institute of Life Insurance, 277 Park Ave., New York 10017.

"Get The Most For Your Dollar On Insurance". *Good Housekeeping,* September, 1974, 176.

"Home Mortgage Insurance." April 1975. Write to U. S. Dept. of Housing & Urban Development, Washington, D. C. 20410.

"How To Read Your Auto Policy". Write to Director, Consumer Information Center, Sentry Insurance, 1421 Strongs Ave., Stevens Point, Wisconsin 54481.

"How To Read Your Homeowners Policy". Write to Director, Consumer Information Center, Sentry Insurance, 1421 Strongs Ave., Stevens Point, Wisconsin 54481.

Kirby, William B, ed. "Life Insurance From the Buyers Point of View". 1974. Write to the American Institute for Economic Research, Barrington, Mass. 01230.

Rodda, W. H. *The Question-and-Answer Insurance Deskbook.* Prentice Hall, 1975.

"Shopper's Guide to Term Insurance"; "Shopper's Guide to Cash Value Life Insurance"; "Shopper's Guide to Health Insurance"; "Shopper's Guide to Mobile Home Insurance". Write to Consumer News, Inc. 813 National Press Building, Washington, D.C. 20045.

"Stretching Your Insurance Dollar". *Business Week,* November 17, 1975, 125–7.

"Your Insurance Program". *Changing Times,* February, 1976, 12.

Investing
The Stock Market

Barron's, published weekly at a cost of $18 a year to the subscriber. Its format is basically the same as the *Wall Street Journal.* It is available on some newstands or write to Dow Jones & Co., 22 Cortlandt St., New York, N. Y. 10007.

Brandt, Catharine. *A Woman's Money: How To Protect and Increase It In the Stock Market.* New York: Cornerstone Library, 1970.

College Classes. Most local colleges and even some night classes held at high schools offer investment courses, designed to acquaint the beginner with the stock market. Check your local college or high school extension board.

Directory which lists hundreds of members of the New York Stock Exchange who are willing to accept small amounts. Send to: Directory, New York Stock Exchange, P. O. Box 1971, Radio City Station, N. Y., N.Y. 10019.

Engel, Louis. *How To Buy Stocks,* 5th ed. rev. Boston: Little & Brown, 1971.

The Exchange Magazine, published monthly by the New York Stock Exchange. $2.50 a year by subscription only. It contains information on investing and the economy. For subscription information write to: The New York Stock Exchange, Investors Service Bureau, 11 Wall St., New York, N. Y. 10005.

Fisher, Robert D. *Manual of Valuable & Worthless Securities,* New York: R. M. Smythe & Co, 13 vols. "showing companies that have been reorganized, merged, liquidated or dissolved; little known companies and oil leases.

Forbes Magazine. $15 by subscription. Published semi-monthly. 60 5th Ave., New York, N. Y. 10011.

Hess, Levy Herta. *What Every Woman Should Know About Investing Her Money,* Chicago: Dartnell, 1968.

Investment Clubs—information including stock selection guides and a portfolio management guide. Write to The National Association of Investment Clubs, P. O. Box 220, Royal Oak, Michigan 48068.

Investment Seminars—These are not uncommon anywhere in the U. S. Watch your local paper or call any brokerage house in your area. For example, in October, 1975, E. F. Hutton & Co. offered a "Workshop For Women—All Day Seminars" in the San Francisco area.

"An Investors Information Kit". $2. Write to Publications Department, New York Stock Exchange, Inc., 11 Wall St., New York 10005.

Loeb, Gerald M. *The Battle For Stock Market Profits.* New York: Simon & Schuster, 1971.

Merritt, Robert D. *Financial Independence Through Common Stocks,* Rev. Ed. New York: Simon & Schuster, 1969.

Moody's, a financial newspaper. Write to Moody's Investors Service, 99 Church St., New York, N. Y. 10007.

Palmer, Hannah Gardner. *How To Be a Woman of Property,* New York: Henry Holt, 1956.

Sederberg, Arelo. *The Stock Market Investment Club Handbook.* Los Angeles: Sherbourne Press, 1971.

Stabler, C. Norman. *How To Read the Financial News,* rev. ed. New York: Harper & Row, 1965.

Standard & Poor's Stock Guide, published Monthly. Rates some 5,000 companies. Also offers statistics about these companies. Write to Standard & Poor's Corp., 345 Hudson St., New York 10014.

Stock Exchanges. There are 13 stock exchanges in the U. S. Any of these can not only offer you printed matter on the workings of the stock market but a tour of the exchange itself. Check the chapter on Stocks for addresses.

"Understanding the New York Stock Exchange". Sept. 1975. Send to: The New York Stock Exchange, Investors Service Bureau, 11 Wall St., New York 10005.

The Wall Street Journal, the financial newspaper. It lists daily the stocks traded on the New York Stock Exchange, the American Stock Exchange and over-the-counter stocks. Printed Monday through Friday, it can be purchased at newsstands or for subscription information write Dow Jones & Co. Inc., 22 Cortlandt St., New York 10007.

"Why Women's Stock Is Rising On Wall Street: Investor Programs At E. F. Hutton & Oppenheimer & Co.". *Business Week,* November 10, 1975, 114+.

Wiesenberger Financial Services. Investment companies. Issued annually. Write to 5 Hanover Square, New York.

Mutual
Funds and Bonds

Barron's, Weekly, $18 a year. Available some newstands or write to Dow Jones & Co., 22 Cortlandt St., New York 10007.

Federal Reserve Bonds. Information on Series H savings bonds. Federal Reserve Banks are located throughout the U. S. Check the chapter on Bonds and Mutual Funds for addresses.

Forbes Magazine. $15 by subscription. Published semi-monthly. 60 5th Ave., New York 10011.

Frank, Robert. *Successful Investing Through Mutual Funds,* New York: Hart, 1970.

Fundscope, published monthly and dealing with mutual fund news. Write to Fundscope, Suite 700, 1900 Avenue of the Stars, Los Angeles, Calif. 90067.

Homer, Sidney. *Bond Buyer's Primer,* New York: Salomon Bros & Hutzler, 1968.

Investment Companies, published annually by Arthur Wiesenberger

Service Division of John Nuveen and Co. Lists most funds, their past and present performance. Obtain a copy in the Reference section of your library.

Johnson Investment Company Charts, published annually. Includes performance charts on all the major funds. Load or no load mutual funds are noted as—load: fee. no load—none/shares offered at net assessed value. This book affords easy comparison between funds through use of charts. It also lists funds, addresses. Obtain a copy in the Reference section of your library.

Markstein, David L. *How To Make Money With Mutual Funds,* New York: McGraw-Hill, 1969.

Moody's, a financial newspaper. Write to Moody's Investors Service, 99 Church St., New York, N. Y. 10007.

Mutual Fund Forum, published bi-monthly by the Investment Company Institute, 1775 K St., N.W., Washington, D.C. 20006. This is the trade publication of most of the funds. It publishes statistics and general information on the industry.

Stabler, C. Norman. *How To Read the Financial News,* rev. ed., New York: Harper & Row, 1965.

Staley, John A. *What About Mutual Funds?* 2nd ed. rev. New York: Harper & Row, 1967.

The Wall Street Journal, the financial newspaper. It lists stocks, bonds and mutual funds traded on the New York Stock Exchange, and the American Stock Exchange. Printed Monday through Friday, it can be purchased at newstands or for subscription information, write Dow Jones & Co. Inc., 22 Cortlandt St., New York 10007.

Writing A Will

Barnes, John. *Who Will Get Your Money?* New York: Morrow & Co., 1972.

Bender, M. "A Problem You Can't Put Off". *McCall's* Magazine, March, 1974, 80+.

Fowler, E. M. "Why Every Parent Needs a Will". *Parents* Magazine, October, 1974, 38.

Gordon, Leland J. and L. James Gordon. "What You Should Know About the Law of Estates". July 1955. Write to The Council on Consumer Information, Ramon P. Hermerl, Executive Secretary, Colorado State College, Greeley, Colorado.

"Planning Your Will". Cooperative Extension Service, Oklahoma State University, Oklahoma City, published in 1970.

Financing Your Way Through a Divorce

Attorney Referral Service. Check your phone book for local office. This service is provided by the local Bar Association. It will suggest an attorney and arrange for you to talk to her or him for one half hour for a nominal fee, before you hire.

Berson, Barbara and Ben Bove. *Survival Guide for the Suddenly Single*. New York: St. Martin's Press, 1974.

Goodman, E. J. "Do-It-Yourself Divorce". *McCall's* Magazine, April, 1974, 35.

Hirsch, Barbara B. *Divorce: What a Woman Needs To Know*. Chicago: Henry Regnery Co, 1973.

Legal Aid Society. Check your phone book for local office. It can refer you to an attorney and in some cases, provide assistance financially.

National Organization For Women (NOW). Check your phone book for local chapter. This organization can supply support, assistance and refer you to an attorney.

Rogers, Harry. *Divorce Without a Lawyer*. Carmel, 1974.

Seldin-Schwartz, E. *"Diary of a Middle-Aged Divorcee"*. *Ms.* Magazine, April, 1976, 84–7+.

Apartments, Cooperatives, Condominiums

"Before You Buy a Mobilehome". Write to Seafire Press, P. O. Box 515, Tustin, Calif. 92680. $1.50. Published in 1971.

"Buying & Financing a Mobile Home". April 1975. Write to U. S. Department of Housing & Urban Development, Washington, D. C. 20410.

Ellis, K. & F. Taddeo. "Condominiums: What They Are, What They Aren't." *Retirement Living,* February, 1976, 30–5+.

"Questions About Condominiums: What To Ask Before You Buy." October, 1974. Write to U. S. Department of Housing & Urban Development, Washington, D. C. 20410.

Skurka, N. "When Less Is More Difficult: Studio Apartments". *New York Times Magazine,* February 15, 1976, 52–3.

Woodall's Mobile Home and Park Directory. $5.95. Check your local bookstore or write to Dept. 240, 500 Hyacinth Place, Highland Park, Ill. 60035. Revised yearly, it rates some 24,000 parks in the U. S.

A House of Your Own

"Basic Housing Inspection". Write to U. S. Department of Health, Education & Welfare, Room 1587, Parklawn Building, 5600 Fishers Lane, Rockville, Maryland 20852.

Groza, Mavis E. "San Francisco: Prestige Home Guide". *San Francisco* Magazine, June, 1975, 77–91.

Mead, S. and others. "What Makes a Good House Great", guidelines. *Better Homes & Gardens,* February, 1976, 44–9.

"Shopping For a House—Here's What To Expect". *U. S. News,* February 2, 1976, 35–6.

"Wise House Buying". September, 1975. Write to U. S. Department of Housing & Urban Development, Washington, D. C. 20410.

Free Insurance Against the Unexpected

Bixby, Lenore E. & Dalmer Hoskins, *Women and Social Security: Law and Policy in Five Countries.* 1973. Write to the U. S. Dept. of Health, Education & Welfare, Room 1587, Parklawn Building, 5600 Fishers Lane, Rockville, Maryland 20852.

"A Brief Explanation of Medicare". Printed by the U. S. Government Printing Office, 1968. No longer available from the Government Printing Office. Refer to copy in local library.

Commissioner of Public Welfare, each state. State welfare information is available on request.

"The Food Stamp Program". Write to the U. S. Department of Agriculture, Food and Nutrition Service, Washington, D. C.

Medicare. Check your local Social Security Office for information, listed under U. S. Government in the telephone book.

State Disability Insurance. Check with your state welfare department.

State Medical Insurance. Check with your state welfare department.

Social Security Benefits. Check your local Social Security Office, listed under U. S. Government in the telephone book.

"Social Security Benefits, including Medicare", 1976. Write to Commerce Clearing House, Inc., 4025 W. Peterson Ave., Chicago, Ill. 60646.

Social Security Disability Insurance. Check with your local Social Security Office, listed under U. S. Government in the telephone book.

Unemployment Benefits. Check with your local State Employment Office.

"Your Claim For Supplemental Security Income", 1968. Write to the U. S. Department of Health, Education & Welfare, Room 1587, Parklawn Building, 5600 Fishers Lane, Rockville, Maryland 20852.

"Your Social Security", November 1974. Write to the U. S. Dept. of Health, Education & Welfare, Social Security Administration, Room 1587, Parklawn Buliding, 5600 Fishers Lane, Rockville, Maryland 20852.

Index